The
Na

C000069847

*How to Identify Covert
Manipulation, Protect
Yourself from Narcissist,
and Recover from
Emotionally Abusive
Relationships*

Jim Covey, PhD.

Table of Contents

Introduction

Abuse in a relationship can be physical or emotional/psychological.

It is easy to recognize the marks of physical abuse; you can't ignore or hide the bruises or contusions in your body. Emotional abuse, on the other hand, can be quite subtle. In fact, you may be in the relationship for years without you realizing that the depression and anxiety you experience are a direct result of the emotional abuse that you are going through.

This is especially true if you are in a relationship with a covert narcissist. A covert narcissist is skilled in emotional control and manipulation. The ways by which he exacts emotional distress and grief on you are subtle. He makes you feel worthless and unlovable, lies to you, and deceives and belittles you in veiled and subtle ways that you do not easily recognize. He also maneuvers situations so that you somehow feel that you are at fault. You fail to recognize that the intense emotional hurt and upheaval you feel are a result of his behavior towards you.

The following chapters enable you to recognize the personality characteristics and behavioral patterns of a covert narcissist. They help you recognize the signs that you are being emotionally controlled and abused. They also give you tools and techniques you can use to protect yourself from the emotional maneuverings of a covert narcissist and to minimize their impact on you. They teach you how to regain self-esteem, optimism, and hope and find your way towards healing and wholeness.

Chapter 1   The Narcissistic Personality Disorder: An Overview

A personality disorder is a mental illness that involves long-term unhealthy and inflexible thought and behavioral patterns.   An individual who has a personality disorder thinks, feels, and behaves in ways that deviate from the normal expectations of the culture. These deviations cause great stress and anxiety. They undermine the individual's ability to function effectively.

A personality disorder requires treatment in one form or another. Without treatment, the symptoms and effects of the disorder can be harmful and long-lasting. They can affect many areas in a person's life including financial affairs, work, family, friendships, and other relationships.

The NPD or narcissistic personality disorder is a type of personality disorder. It is primarily characterized by an inflated sense of self-importance and an excessive need for attention and approbation. This disproportionate focus on the self comes with a lack of sympathy and compassion for other people. Clinical research shows that a self-esteem that is fragile and defenseless against even the slightest suggestion of criticism lies beneath the superficial show of excessive confidence.

A narcissist is an individual suffering from the narcissistic personality disorder. He is excessively self-involved. He is preoccupied with an unhealthy and grandiose sense of self-importance that influences all his decisions, actions, and interactions.

A narcissist shows the following traits and predispositions:

- He has a grand sense of self-importance and success.

- He demonstrates an exaggerated sense of his accomplishments, abilities, and skills.

- He believes that he is a unique and exceptional being and that the world should treat him as such.

- He hungers for recognition, acknowledgement, and esteem.

- He fantasizes about his fame, influence, and self-importance. He is preoccupied with his own success and power, as well as with other people's love and admiration for him.

- He is manipulative. He thinks nothing of exploiting people just so he gets what he wants.

- He has an extreme sense of self-entitlement. He lacks compassion, empathy, and kindness.

- He finds it extremely hard to build and maintain mutually-satisfying relationships.

Psychology describes narcissistic behavior as either overt or covert. Overt behavior is obvious, explicit, and can easily be observed by other people. Covert behavior, on the other hand, is less obvious to other people; it is more restrained and subtle.

You can easily identify an overt narcissist; he tends to stand out in the crowd because of his arrogant, loud, attention-calling, and self-absorbed behavior. A covert narcissist, on the other hand, is less obvious; he tends to be withdrawn or introverted. Some people may even see him as shy, timid, or self-deprecating.

In spite of these obvious differences, however, both the overt and covert narcissists share basically the same traits outlined above. Both are self-absorbed; they go through life unable to regulate their sense of self-importance. Both show a strong predisposition for manipulating other people. Both tend to sow hurt and confusion, particularly in people who love them.

Both overt and covert narcissists suffer from the wide range of symptoms associated with the narcissistic psychological disorder. The people they interact with – spouse, family members, friends, co-workers, and others, are also likely to feel the ill-effects of the person's condition.

The Covert Narcissist

Because of the subtlety of his behavior, a covert narcissist finds it easier to control and manipulate people. You find yourself forming a relationship with such a person without even realizing what kind of person he is. After some time, you come to realize that your interactions lack genuine reciprocity and mutual kindness and love. You experience emotional confusion and pain. In spite of the deep psychological pain, you find it difficult to extricate yourself from the relationship.

Having to deal with a covert narcissist is particularly confusing and hurtful. The emotional manipulation and abuse is hidden and subtle – and usually more sinister and damaging. You suffer from depression and anxiety without realizing that your emotional problems find their source in your relationship with the covert narcissist. You can be in the relationship for years without realizing that you are being emotionally and psychologically manipulated, controlled, and abused.

Chapter 2   Recognizing the Covert Narcissist

Knowledge is power.

Realizing the truth of this adage helps you avoid or minimize the emotional harm and confusion that usually result from being in a relationship with a covert narcissist. If you are able to recognize the general characteristics and behavioral patterns usually associated with covert narcissism, you find yourself in a stronger position. You will be able to navigate and work through the potentially harmful relationship. You will be able to protect yourself from the covert narcissist's manipulations.

The following traits are usually associated with covert narcissism:

- A fragile sense of self that needs to be constantly bolstered by attention and admiration

The overt narcissist is quite obvious about his sense of high-minded superiority. He is bold and arrogant. He wants people to be in awe of him. He wants people to notice and think highly of him and may even demand their constant attention and esteem.

The covert narcissist shares the same elevated feelings of self-importance but may take a less obvious route towards getting the attention he hungers for. He may sometimes purposefully diminish his skills, stature, or accomplishments or give back-handed praise with the shrewd, underhanded design of getting people to praise or admire him for his own talents or abilities.

When he is alone with you, he is condescending. He talks down to you. He always knows best, is much smarter than you, and is always right. He treats you like a doormat– inferior, mediocre, second-rate. He always tells you that your ideas, opinions, and thoughts do not make any sense. He belittles you and makes jokes at your expense. He is always sarcastic and cruel with you.

- The predisposition to blame and shame others

A narcissist blames, shames, and criticizes others as a matter of habit. He is rude and sarcastic. He puts people down so he can feel superior to them. He shames others so he feels the rush of feeling that he is greater, better, and above all of them.

The covert narcissist oftentimes refrains from blatantly shaming you. He makes it appear as if he were a victim. He uses a gentle, subdued approach to make you feel that you are in the wrong and that you are at fault. He seeks to gain leverage by making you feel inept, unworthy, or apologetic.

He always blames you, even for his own mistakes and failings. He doubts everything that you say. He always tries to prove that you are wrong. He tells you that you are stupid.

- The desire to create confusion

A covert narcissist is wily and underhanded in his interactions. He sometimes chooses not to outwardly blame or shame you but to confuse you instead – and make you doubt or second-guess your intentions and actions. He makes you hesitate and entertain misgivings. He does this so he can get the upper hand in the relationship and enjoy the power that it gives him.

He loves to argue for the sake of arguing. He makes ambiguous, conflicting, and confusing statements (sometimes referred to as 'crazy-making'). He nitpicks about everything about you – your work, your cooking, your clothes, and even about your hair.

He has strong, unexpected emotional outbursts and sudden, unexplainable changes in mood. He behaves impulsively and erratically.

- A sense of entitlement and a demanding and critical attitude

He makes unreasonable and irrational demands on you. He wants you to always put him first – to put everything aside just for him. He wants you to spend all your time catering to his needs.

Regardless of how much you try to please him, he is always dissatisfied with everything you do. He is never happy with how much you give or how hard you try. You always fall short of his expectations.

He demands that you think the way he does. You are not allowed to have your own thoughts, opinions, or say on anything.

- A complete disregard for other people's feelings

A covert narcissist is self-focused. He wants all the attention. He looks for opportunities to shine and even manipulates situations so he always comes out ahead of everybody.

He is an expert in making you feel small, insignificant, and unimportant. He may not say this explicitly but his actuations are orchestrated to make you think that your time, interests, and goals are irrelevant. He stands you up on dates. He ignores your suggestions or opinions. He does not respond to your emails or text messages. He does not confirm plans with you and makes it a point to show up late or make you wait.

He invalidates your feelings and distorts your reality. He says that you are 'crazy' or 'too emotional' – and that you always exaggerate or blow things out of proportion. He may even lie about things or deny that situations you refer to even took place.

He refuses to consider your thoughts or feelings as valid. He dismisses or undermines your feelings; he wants to define or dictate how you should feel.

He sees your needs or requests as absurd or ridiculous. He accuses you of being too needy or self-centered. When you try to tell him that you are upset, he challenges you to give him concrete examples, with exact times and dates, about the events that cause you distress. If you fail to do this, he dismisses your feelings as if they mean nothing to him.

- Ineptitude in building and nurturing emotional ties

A covert narcissist is so focused on himself that he is unable to nurture deep, mutually-satisfying emotional bonds with other people. He is so full of himself that he fails to be sensitive or responsive to people who love him.

When you are in a relationship with a covert narcissist, you have to do all the heavy emotional lifting to keep the relationship afloat. He fails to appreciate the good things about you – in fact, he may not even be aware of them. The times where he seems to be emotionally accessible are few and far between. More often than not, his emotional accessibility is just for show. He usually puts up a performance with the end in view of exploiting your emotions and eventually making you feel small and not good enough.

- The predisposition for doing things for self-serving reasons

A covert narcissist is seldom a giver in the true sense of the word. Everything he does is done out of a desire to raise himself up or to get something he wants.

For instance, he tends to do a good deed only when other people are watching or if he is certain he will be noticed, admired, or praised for it. He is motivated to do something good by what he thinks he will get in return. His "kindness" or "generosity" is always about himself; it is never about the person to whom he is being "openhearted" to.

- A controlling and manipulative disposition

He wants to be in total control of you. He tries to isolate you from your friends and family. He wants to be the one to decide which people you see or talk to. He makes fun of the people you love and finds them silly or shallow.

He treats you like he owns you. He coerces you to spend all your time with him. He demands to know your whereabouts at all times.

He is excessively jealous. He accuses you of cheating. He keeps you from being with other people.

He monitors your every actuation and even checks on your email, social media, or text messages. He even hides or takes your car keys so that you are not able to go anywhere without his permission or knowledge.

He uses emotional blackmail to manipulate you. He makes you feel guilty He always goes out of his way to humiliate you. He uses your compassion, values, and fears to control you or to push your buttons. When you do not do as he wants, he ignores you, gives you the silent treatment, and withholds affection.

• Gaslighting behavior

Gaslighting is another characteristic of covert narcissism. The covert narcissist exercises manipulation over you by spinning the truth and spewing deliberate lies. He falsely accuses you in with the end in view of distorting your reality.

Ask yourself the following questions:

Do you feel that you are no longer the same person you were before your relationship with the covert narcissist?

Are you less confident now than you used to be?

Are you more anxious now than you used to be?

Do you find yourself wondering if you are being extraordinarily sensitive?

Do you feel that you can't do anything right?

Do you always blame yourself when things go awry?

Do you find yourself apologizing a lot?

Do you feel that something is not quite right but you can't put a finger to it?

Do you second-guess yourself about your reactions and behavior towards the covert narcissist?

Do you find yourself always making excuses for the covert narcissist's behavior?

If you answered "Yes" to most of the questions, the covert narcissist seems to have successfully manipulated you and made you doubt yourself. Covert narcissists often engage in the manipulative technique of gaslighting as a way to confuse you and distort the way you view reality.

- The incomprehensibly strong need to appear superior to everybody else

A covert narcissist may look timid or modest. Deep inside, though, he has an inordinate sense of self-importance. He wants people to defer to him, to recognize that he is superior to them. As a result, he tends to look down on tasks that he thinks are beneath him. He is also likely to avoid work or social situations that may dispute his sense of superiority.

A covert narcissist usually suffers from social anxiety. He tends to avoid social situations. His desire to always be better than everybody makes him avoid circumstances which may lead to comparisons being made.

A covert narcissist is prone to feel envious and defensive. He is extraordinarily vulnerable to criticism. He tends to see insults where none is given. If he feels that you have slighted him, he is likely to feel vindictive or to act in a passive-aggressive manner towards you.

- Difficulty maintaining effective work relations

A covert narcissist shows behaviors that make it tough for him to sustain smooth and helpful relationships at work. His sense of self-importance keeps him from being an effective team player. He finds it hard to drum up enthusiasm for assignments that he usually sees as far beneath him to do.

Chapter 3   Dating and Falling in Love with a Covert Narcissist

There are many individuals today who are self-centered and self-indulgent. They always put themselves first. They care only about their needs. They are frequently self-absorbed.

When you date a person who posts more than the usual number of selfies on his dating profile, are you dating a narcissist? If your date can't seem to stop talking about himself, is he a narcissist?

Wanting too much attention or being self-absorbed does not always translate into being a narcissist or a person with the clinical mental health condition of narcissism.

The previous chapter outlines the characteristics of a covert narcissist. If you find 5 or more of the following characteristics when you are dating a person, you may want to re-think your position.

Unhealthy need for attention

Exaggerated sense of importance

Conviction that he is special

Sense of entitlement

Being self-absorbed and egotistical

No empathy for other people

Excessive jealousy or envy

Predisposition to emotionally exploit or manipulate other people

Inability to maintain reciprocal or give-and-take relationships

In simple terms, a narcissist is one who is conceited, self-absorbed, and exceedingly insensitive about the feelings of other people. He tends to control and manipulate others.

Covert narcissism is not a black-or-white personality disorder, unlike most mental health conditions. The degree of narcissism usually falls within a spectrum. You usually cannot tell if a person has NPD without the professional judgment of a professionally-qualified specialist.

It is often difficult to recognize a covert narcissist, particularly when you are already romantically or emotionally involved with one. In the first place, when you are dating someone, you usually aren't thinking whether the person has NPD or not. However, it is always prudent to consider whether you and the person you are dating are capable of building a relationship that is healthy and mutually-helpful and whether that relationship will prove to be sustainable in the long term.

It pays to look at any relationship early on. When you find yourself already too emotionally involved with a covert narcissist, you are likely to find it extremely difficult to cut ties. By the time you realize that your relationship with him is not healthy, you are already too caught up in the web that he weaves. By then, you will find it almost impossible to leave the relationship.

Look at the person you are dating and the kind of relationship you have with him. Ask yourself the following key questions. If you find several indications that he has covert narcissistic tendencies, take the appropriate actions to protect yourself.

- Is he very charming (at first)? Does he seem to fall in love with you much too quickly and intensely?

A relationship with a narcissist can look pretty much like a fairytale. A covert narcissist is an expert at 'love bombing.' He floods you with expressions of his admiration and love. He seems convinced that you are well-matched, that you are each other's soul mate and that you are perfect for each other – even when you are just starting to date each other.

According to experts, a narcissist thinks that he is special and that he deserves to be with a person who is also special. He has a peculiar definition of 'special;' it is one who understands and appreciates him completely. Once you do something that disappoints or upsets him, he can turn on you in a really bad and undeserved way.

A narcissist's victim usually has no idea about what she did to deserve a narcissist's 'love' or his 'loathing.' A narcissist's treatment of you is triggered by his own beliefs; it has nothing whatsoever to do with you.

What you should do to protect yourself:

Be wary if a person comes on too strong about how he feels about you even when you have just met each other. If it seems too early for someone to love you, it perhaps is. If it feels like he doesn't know you enough to fall that deeply in love with you, he probably does not. A covert narcissist tends to make up connections, usually shallow and superficial, even when the relationship is just starting.

While it is flattering to have somebody admire or love you from the very beginning, keep in mind that a love that is grown and nurtured is usually love that is real and sustainable.

- Does he dominate the conversation and can't seem to stop talking about how great and amazing he is?

A narcissist, even a covert one, talks incessantly about what a great person he is. He usually does this because of an excessive need to appear self-assured. He needs to feel that he is better or smarter than you and everyone else.

A narcissist always tries to exaggerate his abilities or embroider his accomplishments to get your attention and high regard. He gets too caught up talking about himself that he fails to listen to or to take interest in you. You get a double warning here. First, he does not stop talking about himself. Second, you don't get to talk; you just listen to him.

What you should do to protect yourself:

Try to look more deeply into this. Talk about yourself. Does he seem to want to learn more about you? Does he follow up with questions? Or does he appear not to hear you and simply turns the conversation back to him?

- Does he seem inordinately needy of compliments or praise from you?

Experts say that though a covert narcissist appears self-possessed, he is actually insecure. He has poor self-esteem.

He needs to be praised, to be made to feel good about himself. If you do not give him the praise he needs, he will fish for it. This is why he is persistently looking at you to compliment him and tell him what an amazing person he is.

He uses you to pamper to his sense of self-worth. He needs you to make him feel that he is great. Due to his low self-esteem, however, his ego can be bruised very easily, which just raises his need for praise.

What you should do to protect yourself:

Refrain from complimenting him. As you get to know each other longer, you may notice that he shows signs of frustration when you fail to give him the praise he needs. You may even notice that he resorts to criticizing or putting you down. If you don't lift up a covert narcissist often enough, he tries to lift himself up by putting you down. He is predisposed to punish you for his own lack of self-esteem.

- Does he lack empathy?

The lack of empathy is a hallmark trait of a covert narcissist.

The covert narcissist is unable to make you feel as if he sees, understands, and accepts you. He lacks empathy. He does not know how you feel; he does not even seem interested at all. He fails to validate your feelings.

Experts say that the covert narcissist's lack of empathy is usually the reason why he finds it hard to sustain relationships, whether romantic or not.

What you should do to protect yourself:

When you have had a particularly difficult day, try to share your day and your feelings with the person you are dating. Is he able to sympathize? Does he care when you tell him how another person has made you sad or mad? Does he try to understand where your emotions are coming from? Is he able to validate your feelings?

- He has no (or very few) real and long-term friends.

Many covert narcissists are incapable of nurturing deep and lasting friendships. Because of this, he is likely to feel envious when you spend time with your friends. He tells you that you don't spend enough time with him. He makes you feel guilty. He also criticizes you for your choice in friends. He belittles your friends and makes you feel that you are in the wrong for even wanting to be friends with them.

What you should do to protect yourself:

Look into his connections. Does he talk affectionately about the people in his life? Does he have lifelong friends or does he have only casual acquaintances and buddies whom he constantly trash-talks?

- Do you notice him frequently picking on you?

You may at first think that he is just teasing you when he picks on you. When you do nothing to stop him, however, he does it more frequently.

He seems to enjoy criticizing you unfairly. He disapproves of how you dress, your friends, the shows you watch on TV, and the books you read. Suddenly, he finds something wrong with almost everything about you. He calls you names, hurts you with humiliating remarks, and does things to make you feel bad about yourself.

A covert narcissist does things to lower your self-esteem so that he increases his own. It makes him feel powerful. It makes him feel good to be able to manipulate you and how you feel.

What you should do to protect yourself:

Call him out for his behavior. Let him know that you will not put up with how he is treating you. If he does not change his behavior or, worse, does not see anything wrong with it, you should probably have second thoughts about pursuing the relationship.

- Does he hesitate to define your relationship?

A covert narcissist likes you to treat him as your partner so he can enjoy the intimate emotional and physical benefits that come with being in a relationship. As his partner, he expects you to admire and praise him and build his ego. On the other hand, he remains on the lookout for someone who may be better than you. He thinks nothing about flirting with someone else even when he is with you or people close to you.

When you try to talk to him about how his inappropriate behavior disrespects you, he makes you feel guilty about making a fuss about it. He may say that you are crazy for thinking the way you do and may even use that as a reason for not committing fully to you. On the other hand, if you choose to remain silent about his behavior, he is likely to make you feel that you truly do not deserve his respect. Whatever you do, you are in a lose-lose situation – which is what a relationship with a covert narcissist usually is.

What you should do to protect yourself:

A covert narcissist tends to dance around labeling your relationship. There are a lot of people who do this but if you see this symptom, along with many of the other indications just described, take that as a red flag.

- Does he never apologize? Does he seem to think that he is always right?

It is impossible to win a fight with a covert narcissist. You cannot reason with him; he is not open to compromises. In his eyes, he is always right.

And because he is always right, he does not hear what you are saying. He refuses to understand you. He refuses to take responsibility for his part in any relationship issue. He refuses to compromise.

What you should do to protect yourself:

Take note of the times when he shows up late for your dates or cancels plans at the last minute. Observe how often he fails to keep his promises to you. When you confront him with these behaviors, does he apologize? Or does he fail to see anything wrong with them?

A covert narcissist thinks that he cannot do anything wrong. And because, in his eyes, there is nothing wrong with such behaviors, he does not apologize for them.

Refusing to be in a Relationship with a Covert Narcissist

Experts suggest that if you do decide to end the relationship, do so without discussing it lengthily. Do not argue or try to negotiate. A covert narcissist enjoys pushing your buttons and seeing you react to his manipulations. When you show him that you don't care, you don't give him any power.

Expect him to panic when you try to end the relationship. When a covert narcissist sees you trying to leave him, he gets into a panic. He is likely to try harder to keep you. He reverts back to his initial behavior of love-bombing you. He tries to convince you that he has changed by saying and doing the right things. You may go back to him only to eventually realize that he has not changed at all.

The covert narcissist's tendency to try to win you back can result in an on-again off-again kind of relationship – until you decide to leave him for good or until he finds some other girl to replace you.

He will lash out at you when you stick to your decision to leave him. When you finally decide to have nothing else to do with him, a covert narcissist will make it a point to hurt you for leaving him. He will see your decision as an act of abandonment. His ego will be severely bruised. He will feel that you have wronged him. He will feel anger and hatred for you.

A covert narcissist fails to see his part in making the relationship fail. For him, everything wrong that happens is someone else's fault. In this case, it is your fault. He will bad-mouth you to your friends so he can save face. He is also likely to immediately replace you with someone else not only to arouse your jealousy but to help him restore his ego, as well.

He will try to contact and harass you after he realizes that you are not going back to him. Make a clean break. Block all his efforts to get in touch with you.

Making the Decision

If you are just in the dating stage with a covert narcissist, you are probably not as yet very heavily invested in the relationship. Experts suggest that you get out as soon as you can.

You cannot love a covert narcissist enough. You cannot (and should not) change yourself to meet his expectations. You cannot change him; he will never empathize with you or be in tune with your needs. Your interactions will always leave you feeling inadequate or empty.

A covert narcissist is essentially incapable of building and sustaining a healthy relationship. He will always criticize, belittle, gaslight, and refuse to commit to you. You are likely to find yourself emotionally exhausted. Unless he himself realizes that he needs professional help with his emotional condition – and voluntarily seeks it, it seems farfetched for your relationship with him to prosper into a healthy and mutually-satisfying one.

There are certain things you can do so that the breakup does not take as much toll on your emotional health.

Recognize that you deserve a better partner.

Lean on your healthy relationships with family and friends for support.

Seek the help of people who really know and love you so you are able to keep in touch with your reality.

Do not hesitate to see a therapist if you feel that you need one.

Covert narcissistic behaviors are never acceptable in the context of a loving, healthy, and equitable relationship. If your partner, whether or not he is a covert narcissist, constantly behaves in a way that demeans and humiliates you, it is prudent for you to reevaluate the relationship.

You cannot assume responsibility for how another person behaves. You are, however, responsible for your emotional health and personal wellbeing. You should take care of yourself.

Chapter 4   Living with a Covert Narcissist Mother

The typical mother-child relationship is characterized as a nurturing and unconditionally loving bond. The typical mother is seen as a presence that holds her child's best interests close to her heart. Her actions are always guided by the best intentions – that of guiding, helping, and instructing her child to navigate her way towards meaningful, productive, and happy adulthood.

Unfortunately, not all parent-child relationships take this route.

There are mothers (and fathers) who treat their children with physical and emotional or psychological abuse.

Physical abuse is easily recognized. Emotional abuse, on the other hand, while leaving heavy and usually lasting psychological damage on the victim, can easily fly under the radar.

A mother (or father) is supposed to love, nurture, and support you. A covert narcissist mother, however, can ignore or belittle you, call you names, and heap verbal and emotional abuse on you. She can use subtle and cunning maneuvers to tear down your self-esteem and confidence to make you feel small, hollow, and worthless.

The emotional abuse that you suffer in the hands of a covert narcissist mother often goes undetected for one or more reasons.

The outward signs or the results of the emotional abuse are not as obvious as the physical bruises and welts that a physically abusive parent can render on a child.

A mother may not even realize that what she is doing is wrong. Just because she does not engage in physical abuse, she fails to see the extent of the emotional damage that she is causing her child.

The covert narcissist mother is crafty and cunning. She tears you down emotionally in subtle and underhanded ways that go unnoticed – sometimes, even by you.

A covert narcissist mother is an expert in emotional manipulation. She is capable of acting kind and affectionate in one moment and then subtly changes her behavior to belittle or shame you, undermine your self-esteem, or make you feel guilty. This cycle of behaviors can be hurtful and confusing. Your mother sometimes expresses regret for making you feel bad – and you really want to believe she means what she says. You badly want to forgive her.

Experts say that a covert narcissist is likely to continue with her abusive behavior. Behavioral change is only likely to happen if your mother takes real and significant steps to change her behavior – steps like going to counseling or seeking the help of a therapist.

Seeing Your Mother for Who She Is

Many adult emotional issues find their root in childhood experiences.

Are you having personal and emotional problems and you don't know why? Do you feel incapable of handling emotional issues on your own? Do you suffer from a significant lack of self-esteem and unexplained anxiety? Do you feel small and worthless?

If your mother is a covert narcissist, most of your emotional struggles may stem from your relationship with her.

It might be difficult to understand this initially. You have lived in this manner for years. It is possible to become desensitized to your circumstances. You find it hard to recognize and accept that your relationship is the root of the emotional issues you are grappling with.

A covert narcissist has a remarkable aptitude for emotional deception. For instance, you feel that something is not quite right about your relationship. You discuss the matter with your mother because you want to clear things up and improve the relationship. Instead of listening to your feelings, your mother declares outright that there is absolutely nothing wrong with your relationship. She says that YOU are the problem – that you are making things up or seeing things that are not there. And you end up convinced that she is right. And you continue to feel small and worthless.

The first step to help regain self-esteem and balance is to see your mother for who she is.

Certain typical behaviors are easy to spot in an emotionally abusive covert narcissist mother:

- She is excessively critical of you.

Your covert narcissist mother repeatedly complains about what she sees as your 'faults' and does so in a way that undermines your self-image and makes you feel hurt and belittled. She never acknowledges what you are doing right. She remains blind to your positive characteristics and accomplishments.

In the hands of a covert narcissist mother, feedback becomes a tool for breaking down your self-esteem, your natural sense of self-importance, and the right to advocate for yourself.

Points to consider:

A healthy mother-child relationship includes the space for honesty and constructive feedback. The motivation behind the feedback is to help each other grow and develop. It is motivated by a genuine sense of loving concern. It is backed by generous emotional support.

- She is inconsistent in her responses.

You never know how your mother will react to your behaviors – even to the same behaviors. When you blunder, she can be forgiving at one time - and spiteful and angry at another time.

Points to consider:

People need some sense of consistency and predictability in their relationships.

The mood swings of a covert narcissist mother confuse and hurt you. They frighten you. They make you feel that you are constantly treading on eggshells and that your mother can blow up any time. The constant stress is likely to have significant long-term effects leading to emotional scars.

- She always makes you feel guilty.

She manipulates you by putting you on guilt trips. Her passive aggressive behavior may make it difficult for you to recognize this behavior.

She says things like "Our neighbor is so lucky; her daughter always gives her a call to see how she is doing..." or "Well, you don't visit often enough..." in passing but in a way that consumes you with guilt.

Points to consider:

Mothers often make their children know that they feel sad or neglected but they do so in ways that are not manipulative or passive aggressive. They don't intentionally say things to shame you or make you feel guilty. A covert narcissist mother, on the other hand, wants you to take the brunt of her feelings. She makes you feel responsible for neglecting or failing her. She makes you feel as if you were a 'bad' person – and you don't even know why you feel so negative about yourself.

- She makes you feel responsible for her feelings and behaviors.

When your covert narcissist mother feels despondent, acts out, or explodes in temper, she will not take responsibility for her feelings or actuations. She projects her personal issues on to you and makes you feel undue responsibility and guilt.

Points to consider:

Although you may feel that you have nothing to do with how she acts or feels (her thoughts, feelings, and behaviors are NOT within your control) you may feel unexplainably responsible deep inside. This is how manipulative a covert narcissist mother can be.

- She refuses to talk to you.

A covert narcissist mother uses the silent treatment to tell you that she does not like something about you – the way you treat her, talk to her, neglect her, etc.

She does this to make you feel guilty and to compel you, her child, to make the first move, reach out to her, and make everything right. When her silent treatment succeeds in making you do all these, she feels powerful.

Points to consider:

Even parents can feel frustration every now and then. This does not make it right for them to withhold affection or attention and refuse to talk to their child. It is a parent's responsibility, in fact, to teach her child the value of open communication and of reaching out to each other to build or repair feelings that may have inadvertently been hurt.

- She makes you feel that you are responsible for keeping her happy.

A covert narcissist mother makes you feel that you are responsible for pleasing, soothing, and making her happy. She fails to respect emotional boundaries and tends to over-share her emotional struggles with you and expects you to make everything right for her. She expects you to put everything aside, even your own needs, to accommodate her whims.

Points to consider:

A covert narcissist mother tends to put an unjustifiable load of burden on her child.

Remind yourself of certain truths about your relationship with her: that you may not be ready (or do not want) to do all these things for her, that it does not fall on you to do these for her, that you exercise no control over her emotions, and that you have no role whatsoever in making things go 'wrong' for her.

- She makes you feel inadequate.

Your covert narcissist mother is never satisfied by what you do for her. She does not only criticize you; she is never pleased or content by anything that you do. She always downplays your successes and overstates your mistakes and failures. You can do nothing right.

Points to consider:

When you have to live with impossible standards, you grow up feeling severely disappointed and unhappy with yourself. You feel worthless, even when you are truly successful in your endeavors.

Make the effort to see yourself through levelheaded and compassionate eyes. See to it that you do not end up mirroring your mother's estimation of you.

- She invades your private space.

A covert narcissist mother has no respect for healthy boundaries. In childhood, this lack of respect can take the form of her going through your personal letters and diaries or not allowing you to keep your bedroom door closed. In adulthood, she questions you about your relationships and finances – and expects you to tell her everything. If you refuse to, she gives you the silent treatment and makes you feel bad.

Points to consider:

Everyone wants to have some space for herself. Do not allow your covert narcissist mother to make you feel guilty about your natural and rightful desire for personal space.

It is important that you recognize your mother for the covert narcissist that she is. If you are not able to do this, you will not be able to proceed to the next steps of re-wiring your brain and addressing the emotional problems caused by the relationship.

Chapter 5   Working with a Covert Narcissist

When we talk about an abusive relationship with a covert narcissist, what usually comes to mind are intimate relationships or other domestic scenarios. We immediately think about a husband and wife relationship or a mother and child relationship where the dominant individual metes out emotional abuse to the apparently weaker or defenseless victim.

Emotional abuse from a covert narcissist, however, also takes place in a formal or business-like setting. It can exist in a relationship between professionals in the workplace. And when it does, it can undermine emotional wellbeing, as well as destabilize worker productivity and satisfaction, and lead to high employee turnover.

In many instances, emotional abuse or bullying comes in the form of emotional maltreatment from a covert narcissist boss. However, research shows that emotional abuse can also take place among co-workers – individuals who are supposedly equals or colleagues. This implies that the 'power' factor that is usually at play in a covert narcissist-victim relationship can be attributed to more than just the imbalance that is the result of position or rank. It can also be ascribed to an imbalance in social power.

You sometimes feel that a boss or a colleague is exerting pressure on you in order to establish his dominance. But how do you recognize, in a more definitive way, emotional abuse from a covert narcissist in the workplace -- and what do you do about it?

- The covert narcissist tries to exert emotional control by being verbally and emotionally hostile.

He finds enjoyment in insulting or putting you down. Sometimes, he is openly hostile; his words and gestures leave you in no doubt that he looks upon you with disrespect and disdain. He calls you names and uses insulting language.

Most of the time, a covert narcissist tends to be sly or covert in the way he makes you feel his scorn. He shows his feelings about you in a more indirect and roundabout way. He pretends to be civil by saying nice words about you but his facial expressions and body language contradict what he says.

He talks behind your back to your co-workers and tries to sway them to criticize or reject you the way he does. He uses this behavior to establish his superiority over you.

He is also adept at giving you the silent treatment as a way to toy with your emotions. He does not even try to explain why he is being unresponsive to you. He wants you to feel insecure and lose your confidence, composure, and concentration at work. He wants to sabotage your efficiency and performance.

What should you do?

Stay calm. Keep your behavior decent and civil. Do not lose your temper. This is exactly what the covert narcissist wants you to do. He feeds off your uneasiness and misery. He is provoking you to annoy you and to get you to react angrily.

If you find it difficult not to lose your cool, walk away. Practice mindful breathing. Do not try to talk to him until you have regained your composure.

When you talk to your covert narcissist abuser, do so in a rational and confident manner. Look him straight in the eye. Talk to him where other employees (especially those who have witnessed his abuses) can see you.

Ask the covert narcissist in plain and simple language to stop his disrespectful and inappropriate behavior. Talk in a self-assured and unemotional manner. Tell him firmly that you will not stand for what he is doing. Inform him that if he does not stop, you will have no recourse but to make an official report about the incidents. (Be proactive by documenting all the details of the abusive acts, as well as your efforts to amend the situation to strengthen the impact of your report).

Point out why his behaviors are inappropriate. More often than not, a covert narcissist will rile you into reacting by attacking personal matters or your private life. If this is true with your abuser, tell him that he is being unprofessional. He is wrong to attempt to mix your personal life with workplace matters. By saying this, you are setting boundaries and showing your abuser -- and the people you work with – that you are serious about keeping personal and professional matters separate.

- He does not only give you the silent treatment; he totally shuts you out so that you feel alone, rejected, and isolated.

The covert narcissist tries to keep you out of social gatherings and functions that involve the people at work. He sees to it that you are not invited. If you are invited, he does everything he can so that other people ignore you or leave you alone. For example, if there are plans for a work-related planning conference or a teambuilding workshop, he will initiate action or use his wiles or position to exclude you. He may even intercept memos or messages so you don't get to find out about the event until it is over.

In conversations, he rebuts everything that you say. He shoots down your ideas as not feasible; he does not listen to you or make faces to show you and your co-workers that he thinks that your ideas are silly or contemptible. He may even treat you as if you do not exist. He wants to make you realize that you are a wrong fit for the company. He makes you feel uncomfortable, miserable, and out of place. He behaves in ways that tell you that he has no respect for your ideas or feelings.

What should you do?

Be direct, confrontational, and straightforward. Initiate a dialogue. Ask him why he is acting the way he is. Ask him to stop.

The covert narcissist wants to make you feel isolated and alienated. When you come forward to ask him to discuss the situation head on, he is likely to feel discomfited by your effort to make him see you. Your tough-talking approach makes him realize that you will not take his behavior lightly. He will think twice about doing the same again.

If you do not feel that you have the mental toughness to do this, get the courage to at least approach a neutral party (like your supervisor or a close colleague) to talk in your behalf. In the meantime, look for ways to grow in confidence and mental fortitude so you find the strength to approach the covert narcissist the next time.

- He instills fear and tries to intimidate you.

A covert narcissist who holds a supervisory or managerial position in the workplace will try this tactic to control or manipulate you. He tries to wield control over you in the guise of asserting his professional authority over you. He cows you into emotional submission and you end up feeling worthless, timid, and terrified.

A covert narcissist humiliates and ridicules you while making it appear that he is teaching you and motivating you to perform better at your job. He makes a big show out of 'coaching' and 'motivating' you while he is, in fact, making you feel incapable and inept. He also seeks to make you look bad to management.

A covert narcissist constantly breathes down your neck to make you feel incompetent, demoralized, stifled, and suffocated. He wants you to feel small. He wants to put you on edge all the time and increase your stress and anxiety by his continuous intimidation.

What should you do?

If you feel brave enough, which is not highly likely (covert narcissists usually choose for their victims people who they think are not likely to complain or confront them), you may want to confront your abuser. Otherwise, get an objective party to represent you. This action will make the covert narcissist realize that you will not take the situation sitting down. It tells him that you will not keep quiet about what he is doing and that you will ask for help and let other people know about his inappropriate behavior.

A covert narcissist has an abnormal need to have other people look at him with high regard and admiration. If you make him realize that you will not hesitate to lay the emotional abuse out in the open, he is likely to backpedal and rethink his ways.

Some people take legal action, especially when the covert narcissist's method of intimidation makes them fear for their safety. Before you take this line of action, see to it that you have a record of the incidents of emotional abuse. Record all the essential details like dates, witnesses, the acts of emotional abuse, and the effects of the abuse on you.

- A covert narcissist minimizes and denies the emotional abuse and even puts the blame on you.

A covert narcissist is an expert at emotional manipulation. He refuses to admit to his wrongdoings. In the first place, he feels entitled; he is convinced that he has the right to behave in whatever manner he sees fit.

He is also self-absorbed. He is insensitive to how his inappropriate behavior makes you feel. All he cares about are his own interests.

When you confront him about his behavior, he tends to make light of it. He remains uncaring and nonchalant about everything. He will even say that you are just making up stories or making mountains out of molehills.

He makes you feel that you are, somehow, to blame for the situation you find yourself in. If you suffer from low self-esteem, you eventually believe that it is, indeed, your fault.

What should you do?

Talk to the covert narcissist about his inappropriate behaviors and how he has to change them. It is prudent to have a superior stand witness to the discussion and to act as a mediator should intervention be required.

Stay calm. Even if the covert narcissist tries to break down your defenses, stay in control of your emotions. Even if the covert narcissist is persuasive and eloquent, do not accept the blame that he is trying to pin on you. When someone inflicts emotional abuse, he makes a conscious decision to do so. He is not 'forced' to do it or 'coerced' or 'led' into doing it.

Chapter 6   Healing From Emotional Abuse: Recognizing the Stages

You do not heal from an emotionally abusive relationship easily. You go through stages – and may backslide every now and then. There may even be times when you take a couple of strides forward one time and then slip back three steps the next. You grapple with self-doubt on occasion and sometimes take significant leaps with hopeful anticipation at other times.

No matter how insignificant the progress may seem like at times, keep on pushing yourself forward. Staying in an emotionally abusive relationship is not an option. You don't deserve the abuse; no one does.

As the previous chapters show, a relationship with a covert narcissist does not always have to be romantic in nature. There are a lot of individuals who suffer from narcissistic abuse from their spouse or partner; there are also individuals who fall prey to the narcissistic maneuverings of a mother, a boss, or a friend. The process of recovery from emotional abuse is similar, regardless of who instigates the emotional abuse.

If you are a victim of narcissistic abuse, expect to go through the following stages of realization and healing:

1. Distress and denial

Once you suspect that you are dealing with a covert narcissist, you go through emotions of shock, distress, and denial. Your mind tries really hard to renounce the evidence that supports the realization.

"He is not a narcissist. He may have a great number of flaws and incapacities when it comes to expressing his love (or respect) for me but he DOES love me! Maybe if I try harder to please him, he will be able to accept and love me as he should, to acknowledge me for the person that I am, to give me the attention and respect that I deserve..."

Initially, you struggle to face the indications that your partner (or boss, best friend, or mother) is a covert narcissist. You find yourself loathe to admit the possibility. After all, you have been with him for quite some time. While you realize that the relationship has known more downs than ups, you keep hoping that things will take a turn for the better. You keep on giving your partner excuses for his behavior.

"He seemed thoughtful in the beginning; maybe, he will be again. Maybe he is just too stressed out... or too busy...or too preoccupied with work... Well, of course, he is not perfect! Nobody is. Maybe I am expecting too much from him. Maybe all relationships do turn sour or boring or unfulfilling. Maybe it is my fault that I am always unhappy..."

Even when you constantly try to explain away his indifference and seeming lack of love and respect for you, you will discover that you can't get rid of the niggling doubts and misgivings.

2. Pain and guilt

As you begin to see your partner for who he is and become painfully aware of the covert narcissistic traits he possesses, you start blaming yourself for allowing yourself to become involved with him. You feel guilty for not seeing the red flags. You feel responsible for being part of a relationship that is characterized by manipulation and control.

You feel the pain come in a rush. You have wasted time, energy, and effort in trying to make the relationship work. You have always put his desires and needs first. You have always listened to him and given him attention – even to the extent of losing your real self. You have given up your life trying to make his life happy.

"This is my fault! How could I be so blind and stupid? I spent all these years trying to please him. I have invested in him all the love and emotion I am capable of giving. I tried to believe in him, to make excuses for him. Now I feel remorse, pain, and guilt that I allowed him to seduce me into putting up with his crap! I only have myself to blame for the miserable situation I am in."

3. Resentment and bargaining

As you go through the stages leading to healing, you start to feel a healthy and righteous anger toward your partner. However, the hope that you can still make things right will rear its head again and again.

"I am so angry with him! He has seduced, manipulated, and misled me! But maybe there is still hope...? If I keep on trying, maybe I can still get him to change. If I continue to put up with him, to sacrifice my needs for what he wants, maybe there is still a chance that I will get the love and respect that I deserve...?"

It is at this stage that you should keep reminding yourself that a narcissist is unlikely to change unless he reaches crisis point or he sees a clear advantage in it for him. If you decide to wait for him to change so that he sees things from your point of view, you may just be wasting your time and energy.

A covert narcissist is hard-put to empathize with people. He is incapable of seeing things from a perspective other than his own. He can even turn things around and make it appear that he is the victim in this relationship. Do not allow him (again) to make it about him.

4. Loneliness, depression, and reflection

This stage may be one of the most difficult stages of healing. It is prudent if you have someone you trust with you to support and encourage you so you don't go through this stage alone.

"I have always been compassionate, loving, and understanding towards him. I have always tried to be honest and true to him. I have always put him first. And he does nothing but to betray and exploit me. Now I feel bereft and empty. He has never really loved me; I realize this now. Everything I have done has been for nothing. Will I be able to trust and love again?"

This is the time where you reckon with and get to fully understand the immense problems that come with having a covert narcissist play a crucial role in your life. You process strong and difficult emotions. You finally understand the trauma that you are going through. This process is usually slow, intricate, and painful. However, it allows you to learn, get to know yourself once more, grow, and cope.

5. The upward turn for the better

"There is always hope. There are good people – people who will not exploit my vulnerability and compassion. I have friends who really care for me. They have always been there for me. They love and accept me for who I am. They are not there just to manipulate or take advantage of me. I know that I am worthy – of love, respect, and kindness. I will find strength in myself and in the people who truly care for me."

This is the stage where things look hopeful. After coming to terms with the reality of your unhealthy relationship, you feel free; you feel better about yourself and about life in general.

You realize that not everyone in your life is a covert narcissist. You feel ready to trust again. You feel hopeful about relationships. You feel ready to let go of people who are using you and to start investing your energy in people who are able to reciprocate your love and kindness.

6. Working through and rebuilding

You are now able to accept the need to let go. You also recognize that the unhealthy and debilitating relationship you have been in is not entirely your fault. You recognize your vulnerability; you know that you have allowed yourself to be controlled and manipulated. You take responsibility for this. However, you also recognize your partner's culpability. He has taken advantage of you. He is also responsible – even more so than you are.

You know that you can't change him. You do not take the blame or the responsibility for his emotional problems and disruptive behavior.

It is at this stage where you try to gain more insights into your own behavior. Why did you put up with the unhealthy relationship? What needs made you vulnerable? How can you be stronger the next time around? How can you strengthen your sense of self so that you are not as susceptible to other people's emotional manipulations?

7. Acceptance and hope

"I accept my mistakes. I know that I can do better. I have the strength to learn from the experience and to learn to trust and love again."

"I will rebuild my life. I am open to the possibility of finding a reciprocal relationship with someone who is able to cherish and value me in the same way that I appreciate and value him. I look forward to becoming more self-aware, assertive, and positive about myself. I will not put myself in the position of being controlled and made to feel small or worthless again."

Reinforce your inner confidence by developing the abilities you need to keep yourself from being controlled and manipulated by other people. Aim to grow in self-awareness. Recognize your needs and desires and look for healthy ways to fulfill them. Nurture self-compassion. Know that you are a person of value, worthy to give and receive love.

The journey towards healing is long, gradual, and difficult. You will see spurts in growth and success. You will experience failure. You will go through days where nothing seems to be happening. Carry on regardless of the circumstance. Keep a hopeful and positive attitude. Be kind to yourself. Keep your focus on becoming healed and discovering your authentic self once more.

Chapter 7   The Importance of a Social Network

Social support refers to material and psychological help that people you know (often referred to as your social network, including family, friends, co-workers, members of your religious community, social organizations, therapist, etc.) provide to help you cope with stress.

Support comes in many forms, including financial assistance, help in daily tasks, advice or counsel, or expressions of concern, care, and empathy. It implies that you enjoy a sense of belonging or a certain degree of intimacy or emotional openness to these people.

Life with a covert narcissist can be rough and emotionally exhausting. Your social network helps by giving you the emotional support that you need to cope with the situation that you are in. They are there to offer a shoulder to cry on, encouragement when things get really bad, companionship to get you through feelings of loneliness, and the reassurance that you are not alone. They give you strength.

In other instances, your social network provides instrumental support. They help you out with your physical needs and offer assistance for tasks that require outside help. They help address your immediate needs. Your mom prepares you a casserole when you are sick. Your sister buys you your groceries. Your best friend drives you around when your car is in the repair shop.

Informational support, on the other hand, comes in the form of information, guidance, and mentoring or advice. This is particularly important when you have to make life-changing decisions or prepare to make big changes in your life.

Having a circle of people who are ready to give you support helps ease the anxiety and stress associated with having to live with a covert narcissist. It is reassuring, comforting, and empowering to have these people in your life.

Making Room for Family and Friends in Your Life

As a victim of emotional abuse, you usually do not want to talk to people about what you are going through.

Being in an emotionally abusive relationship shakes your trust in people. You feel unworthy, unloved, and rejected. You stand in constant fear of being criticized, judged, and neglected.

These fears tend to make you want to isolate yourself from family and friends.

Research shows, however, that this is the time that you need the presence of other people the most. You need to connect with people.

Being with people makes you feel less isolated and lonely. It helps you make sense of life. It helps you see things in perspective.

Healthy and fun relationships increase your sense of worth. They make you feel appreciated and valued for who you are. They make you feel that you belong.

Having fun interactions with other people also reduces stress. It promotes the release of dopamine, the 'happy' neurotransmitters responsible for feelings of happiness.

It you can't get yourself to share what you are going through, start with small friendly interactions. Have lunch with a friend you have not spoken to for quite some time. Watch a movie with your sister. Even when you feel like staying home, accept an invitation to a party. Look for a new social hobby so you can make new friends. When you spend time with friends, you also put some emotional distance from the covert narcissist in your life.

It doesn't take much to build a social network. Go for coffee breaks with a co-worker. Have quick chats with your neighbor. Talk to your best friend on the phone. Do volunteer work. Interactions that start small may grow into meaningful relationships that last.

Recovering from an emotionally abusive relationship is extremely difficult. It helps if you have someone on your side to help you go through your daily challenges.

Building and Strengthening Your Network of Social Support

Keep at least a few confidantes and friends in your life. Having social support helps build your confidence in many ways. It improves your ability to cope with stress and anxiety. It alleviates the harmful effects of emotional distress. It promotes good mental and emotional health. It increases self-esteem. It promotes positive lifestyle behaviors. It encourages you to take action to promote self-care.

How do you build your social network? Here are some practical ideas to help you:

> Nurture your relationships with family and friends.

Make them know how much they mean to you. Show them that you appreciate them. Always say "thank you" for everything they do for you, no matter how small.

Reciprocate their love and concern. Give back. Make yourself available during the times when they need your presence and support.

Keep in touch. Return their emails, Answer their phone calls. Respond to their invitations. Let them know that you are thinking of them.

Be happy for them. Don't compete or feel envious. Rejoice with them when they succeed.

Practice active listening. Be really interested in what they are saying.

Choose to be with people who genuinely know you for who you are.

Do not buy into the covert narcissist's version of who you are. It is a distorted picture. A narcissist does not see the real you. Maybe he is incapable of doing so or intentionally 'distorts' how he sees you.

People who care for you provide a clear and honest reflection of your true self. They help you maintain perspective. They allow you to validate your thoughts and emotions. Choose to spend time with them.

If the covert narcissist in your life has somehow kept you from your circle of family and friends (some narcissists do this to gain better control), re-establish your connection with them. Rebuild erstwhile friendships. Reconnect with people who respect you and listen to you – people with whom you don't have to pretend, with whom you feel that it is okay to be yourself.

Do volunteer work.

Choose a cause that resonates with you and get involved. Helping other people keeps you from over-focusing on your problems. It is also a good opportunity to meet friends who share your values and interests.

Find meaningful pursuits, productive work, and interesting hobbies.

Everyone needs emotional support. A covert narcissist is unable to give you this. You have to look for it somewhere else – in friends and family. In like manner, everyone seeks personal fulfillment, a purpose to one's efforts. A covert narcissist is also unlikely to be a good source for this. Look for it in new hobbies and other meaningful pursuits.

Take a class. Find interesting hobbies. Learning something new is good for your morale. Being busy and productive also enhances self-esteem.

Keeping active by pursuing work, hobbies, and other interests gives your life purpose and meaning. It allows you to develop skills, use your talents, and nurture your abilities. It enhances your self-esteem.

Join a jogging group or a fitness gym. The physical exercise is good for you. It is also a good way to meet people.

The Importance of Having Someone on Your Side

People in emotionally abusive relationships find it tempting to avoid interacting with other people.

Do not give in to your inclination to bottle up your pain and keep your troubles to yourself. Keep in mind that the lack of social interaction and support makes things worse. It lowers your immune system and undermines your physical health. It increases your feelings of loneliness. It undercuts your mental and emotional strength.

When you don't have anybody you can confide in, you feel lost, forlorn, and isolated from the rest of the world. You feel weak and vulnerable. If you have someone to talk to, on the other hand, you feel reassured. You are able to decompress and unload your thoughts and insecurities. You have someone to tell you that you are not going crazy. You have someone to encourage you and give you strength to hang on.

People who have stayed in unhealthy relationships for quite some time tend to find a certain degree of familiarity with the pattern of dysfunction. Do not allow yourself to be lulled into thinking that your relationship is acceptable just because it is familiar. Remind yourself that your relationship makes you feel small. It makes you lose touch with who you really are. It stifles you. It does not allow you to grow. It even belittles you. It makes you feel unnaturally ashamed and guilty. It is bad for you.

If you find yourself emotionally ready for deeper interpersonal exchanges, spend time with those who support and love you. Although you may not initially find it viable, find the mettle to get yourself to tell someone you trust about what you are going through. Putting the pain that you are experiencing into words helps to make it a bit lighter. Sharing your pain and confusion with a confidante helps alleviate the agonizing feeling of being lonely and cut off.

You shouldn't force yourself to do anything that you don't feel comfortable doing. If you don't feel like sharing everything that is happening to you, that is quite all right. The mere knowledge that someone who cares about you knows that you are in pain will help lighten the burden.

It also helps to find one or a couple of trusted family members or friends who are able to listen to your story without judgment. When you have people who treat you with understanding and compassion, it makes it easier for you to find the pluck to do the right thing.

Having a group (it doesn't have to be big) of co-workers, friends, or family members you can count on for support is critical for getting you through the tough times. It helps to greatly enhance your quality of life. It is comforting (and empowering) to know that you have people who will be there for you whenever you need them.

Chapter 8   Setting Boundaries

A covert narcissist finds it hard to respect healthy boundaries. He is self-focused. He has a strong sense of entitlement. He does things for self-serving reasons. He looks at boundaries as something that interferes with his goals. They get in his way. When you set boundaries, you are, in effect, telling him that his tactics do not work with you.

Personal boundaries are essential to emotional wellbeing. They enable you to maintain a positive self-image. They demonstrate to everyone, including yourself, that you have self-worth and self-respect - and that what other people want or expect from you do not define you.

Personal boundaries are limits (physical, mental, and emotional) that you set for self-protection and safety. They keep others from using, manipulating, or violating you. They separate who you are, your thoughts and feelings, from other people's thoughts and feelings. They enable you to express yourself as an individual, unique and with distinct needs, emotions, values, and preferences. They also make you respect the boundaries that other people set for themselves.

Healthy boundaries establish that you are in control of your thoughts, feelings, choices, attitudes, and behaviors. They enable you to become aware when others try to wrest control of them from you. In the same manner, they also tell you when others hold you responsible for their thoughts, feelings, choices, attitudes, and behaviors - things that you are NOT responsible for.

When you establish healthy personal boundaries, you keep your integrity. You acknowledge that you are responsible for who you are. You are in control of yourself and your wellbeing.

Personal boundaries are essential to healthy relationships. They nurture self-respect, as well as respect for others. By marking the physical and emotional lines that govern a relationship, they create a healthy sense of relational confidence, predictability, and safety.

Healthy boundaries promote mutual respect, love and caring. They allow for two people to thrive - as individuals and as a healthy, harmonious, and reciprocal unit.

A covert narcissist does not understand the concept of true reciprocity in your relationship. He does not see or hear you, except as someone who can fulfill his needs. Because of this, he fails to recognize healthy boundaries or deliberately ignores and disrespects them. And he does so without hesitation or remorse. He does so out of a sense of entitlement.

A covert narcissist feels entitled to go through or to use your things without asking. He thinks nothing about going through your personal correspondence or reading your email. He eavesdrops on your conversations. He barges in, cuts you short when you are speaking, and disrupts what you are doing without any second thought.

He steals your ideas. He gives unsolicited advice and opinion. He even dictates how you should feel or think.

It is essential for you to see these actions as violations of your boundaries and rights. You need to establish personal boundaries, communicate these boundaries to him, and uphold and sustain them. It is essential for your wellbeing. At times, it can even be lifesaving.

Why Do You Find It Difficult to Set Limits?

Not everyone finds it easy to set boundaries.

The ability to establish boundaries and to stand your ground about them is associated with a number of positive characteristics. It is linked to emotional maturity. It demonstrates the willingness to accept personal responsibility for the choices that you make in life. It reflects the capacity for emotional autonomy. It reflects self-sufficiency.

Why then is it difficult to set boundaries when you have a person in your life who suffers from covert narcissism? Why do you choose to stay in a cruel and hurtful relationship? Common reasons include the following:

You feel that you have nowhere to go.

A covert narcissist is particularly gifted when it comes to exploiting your vulnerability. He has perfected the art of deception and manipulation. He knows exactly what buttons to push. He knows what to say to exploit your emotional weaknesses and fears.

Some people say that when you find yourself in a relationship with a covert narcissist, you are in a catch-22 situation. Catch-22 refers to an impossible situation, a situation with no way out because its solution is also its cause. You find yourself trapped; there seems to be no way of escape.

Many victims of covert narcissists are weak emotionally for one reason or another. They tend to feel that they are unlovable. They have poor self-esteem. Some may be weak because they are by nature constitutionally predisposed to being emotionally fragile. Some may be weak because of cultural factors. Still others may be weak because of early childhood experiences like parental abuse.

When you are emotionally delicate, you are more open, more susceptible, to finding yourself in a relationship with a covert narcissist who treats you badly. When you find yourself being treated in an unloving, unkind, and hurtful way, you become more convinced that you are, indeed, unworthy of being loved. The more worthless or unlovable you feel, the less likely you are to walk out of the relationship.

You are afraid to set boundaries because you think that if the narcissist oversteps these boundaries, you can't do anything about it. Your hands are tied. You have nowhere to go. You feel trapped because you feel certain that nobody else will consider you worthy.

You think you can't outsmart him.

Most covert narcissist are very, very good at what they do – making you feel unworthy, vulnerable, and weak. Even if you try your best to outwit him, to anticipate his plans and outmaneuver them, you feel that you simply can't keep up. You don't know how. He continues to confound, outsmart, and exploit you. So you simply give up.

You are in denial.

You find yourself in such a bad situation that your mind simply refuses to see it for what it is. If the convert narcissist takes advantage of you and abuses your goodness and your love, it is possible for you to pretend to yourself that none of it is happening. In spite of the clear signs that you are being maltreated, you try to overlook or explain them away. You need to keep up the pretense so you can maintain your feelings of self-worth.

You think you can 'fix' things.

This usually happens when you enter the relationship when you are young and still full of dreams and idealism.

You feel bold, hopeful, and invincible. You think you can do anything you put your mind to. So you stay in the relationship believing that you can make the covert narcissist change.

The covert narcissist helps you maintain this outlook (and gets you to stay with him) by acting nice every now and then. The use of intermittent reinforcement is potent. You see that he is sometimes good to you – and you believe that you can do things that can make him 'be good' more often.

You are afraid to offend him.

You feel that he is your whole world, your only world. You don't want him to shun you so you will do anything, even at the expense of ignoring your own needs, to please him. You panic at the thought that you might no longer be given the 'crumbs' of his pseudo-approval and pseudo-love.

You are afraid that he will punish you.

You accept behaviors that seem to be out of line because you fear that he is going to act much worse if you say "No."

As long as your life is not in danger, you can set boundaries and say "No." Say it without drama. Say it firmly – and mean it. Walk away if you have to. See him in YOUR terms.

There is no clear-cut formula for effectively setting boundaries. However, even the slightest effort to set limits can make things better and more hopeful.

The ability to set your own boundaries and recognize those of others is a precondition for mental health. If you are involved with a covert narcissist, whether personally or professionally, you have to try to establish boundaries and get him to respect them. You owe it to yourself.

How to Set Healthy Personal Boundaries

Use the following techniques to establish boundaries:

1. Know that it is your right and responsibility to set boundaries.

You must hold yourself responsible for how you let other people treat you. When you set and uphold healthy, clear, and decisive personal boundaries, you are telling people what you see as acceptable in your life and what you consider unacceptable. You define, protect, and nurture yourself. You recognize that you – and not the people in your life, are the source of your sense of identity and your self-worth.

2. Be clear about the behaviors that you will not tolerate in other people.

78

You have to identify behaviors that you don't find acceptable – and let others know about these limits.

When dealing with your partner, for example, you may want to establish the following limits:

I will not let you shame, demean, or humiliate me.

I will not let you threaten or curse me.

I will not let you control, manipulate, or force me to do things against my will.

I will not let you belittle how I think or feel.

I will not let you unashamedly ignore, disregard, or disrespect my opinions.

I will not let you become so selfish that you find it okay to dismiss my legitimate needs without thinking twice about them.

I will not allow you to cut me off from my family and friends.

I will not let you appropriate my money, phone, car keys, and other essential personal belongings.

I do not find it acceptable for you to behave in a manner that is so unreasonably and excessively jealous or possessive that it undermines my dignity, hampers my basic freedom, and destabilizes my peace of mind.

I will not let you throw things at me or push or beat me.

I will not remain silent when you abuse me. I will get the appropriate help if the situation demands it.

When a person crosses the line, disrespects you, or behaves inappropriately, tell him. Don't hesitate to let others know when you need physical and emotional space. Be clear about what you intend to do if someone deliberately and maliciously disrespects your limits.

3. Believe and trust in yourself.

Recognize that there is no higher authority on you than you. Nobody knows yourself better than you do. You are your best advocate. You know exactly what is best for you; you know your needs, values, and preferences.

Make your own decisions. Acknowledge your abilities and strengths. Respect your individuality.

When you allow yourself to become needy, to play the victim, or act as if you need others to rescue you, you undermine your boundaries.

4. Make a plan.

After you have created and stated your boundaries, it is important that you follow through. This can be intimidating and even terrifying, especially if you have been in a long-standing relationship with a covert narcissist.

Improve your chances for success by making a plan of action. Keep your goals in mind. Anticipate the potential problems and complications.

What important changes in your relationship do you want to accomplish? How do you intend to enforce your boundaries this time?

Were there techniques that you tried in the past that were successful? Can you use them again? Try to recall the techniques that didn't work so you can avoid them this time. How do you assess the balance of power in your relationship right now? How will this affect your plan?

The answers to these questions may help you appraise the options available to you and help you come up with a realistic and workable plan of action.

5. Be assertive.

Asserting yourself can be quite scary, especially if you are not accustomed to doing it. Remind yourself why you are doing this. Although what you are doing is a clear departure from your usual behavior, it is time that you advocate for yourself. By affirming your boundaries, you let people know that you value and respect yourself. You are asserting your dignity and self-respect. You are watching out for your wellbeing and peace of mind.

When you have been under the influence of a covert narcissist for quite some time, you feel that you are no longer in command of your own life. The emotional control he enjoys over you can be so strong that you feel defeated and totally useless and insignificant.

If you are to recover and fully heal from the toxic relationship, you have to learn to assert yourself. You must assert yourself, consider your needs and desires a priority, so that you gain back the sense of control that everyone should have over his own life.

What is assertiveness?

Assertiveness is being able to express who you are without feeling anxious or stressed out about doing so – and being able to do so in ways that do not breach other people's rights. It is feeling free to honestly articulate your feelings, thoughts, rights, opinions, and attitudes without violating the rights of other people.

Assertiveness is taking responsibility for who you are – and for your life. This is easier said than done, particularly if you have been in a relationship characterized by emotional abuse. Here are a few strategies which may help you in your personal journey to becoming more assertive:

Take a long, close look at yourself vis-à-vis your ability to assert yourself.

Are you absolutely lacking in assertiveness? Or do you find it easy to express your thoughts and feelings about certain matters but cannot for the life of you do the same about other issues? Are you assertive with some people but meek, diffident, and unsure with others? In what areas in your life are you too aggressive, too passive, or just-right assertive? Think about the specific ways you can use to be more assured and confident about expressing yourself. Start working on being more assertive.

Take responsibility for your life. Recognize that you are in control. Face your challenges. Clean up your own messes. Take credit for your achievements.

Do not assume responsibility for other people's feelings and behavior. Recognize that the feelings, wishes, and behavior of other people, even those that you love, are their own responsibility and lookout. Take responsibility for how you feel and behave – and let others do the same thing for their own feelings and behavior.

When someone asks for your preference or opinion, do not hesitate to give it.

What do you want to eat tonight? Where would you want to go? What movie would you want to watch? When someone asks you these questions, do not hesitate to answer. Articulate your desires. The same goes for your opinion. Do not be too meek or compliant. There is a difference between being nice and being docile.

Learn to say "No." Do not inconvenience yourself for other people all the time. Say "No" when it is necessary. It is a sign of a healthy and mutually-nurturing relationship.

Put in the necessary practice-time. Everything gets better with practice – even the application of assertiveness. Give your opinion. Open up about what you feel. Speak out. If the thought of asserting yourself scares you, choose to practice with people who know what you are going through. Pick out 'safe' situations in which to practice.

Watch your body language. It reflects and broadcasts how you really feel deep inside.

When showing assertiveness, reinforce what you say with the appropriate body language. Always stand straight and tall. Maintain eye contact. Use appropriate hand gestures to make a point.

Develop your social skills. People who have been in emotionally abusive relationships tend to keep to themselves. They shy away from being with people. They are reticent, uncomfortable, and unsure of themselves.

Work on your social skills. Read self-help books about the subject matter. Get a socially outgoing friend to teach and help you. Get out on the field and interact with people.

6. Use a calm and gentle approach.

Keep in mind the kind of person that you are dealing with and tread carefully. When you point out his dysfunctional, unacceptable, or hurtful behavior, you challenge his self-image, as well as his feelings of importance and superiority. You may antagonize him. Asserting your limits may increase the tension in the relationship.

Talk in a calm, gentle, and respectful manner. Focus on your feelings. Tell him how his behaviors make you feel; do not mention the intention or motivation behind his behaviors.

If the covert narcissist becomes extremely emotional, defensive, or angry, stay calm. If nothing you say seems to defuse the emotional heat, walk away temporarily. Tell him that it might be better for both of you to calm down first and resume the conversation later.

7. Be firm.

It is useless to set boundaries if you are not willing to uphold them. Your partner is likely to rebel against the limits that you set. He will test your resolve. You have to be prepared for this.

Tell him firmly what you will do if insists on behaving in unacceptable ways. For example, tell him that if he keeps on insulting you or calling you names, you will not carry on with the conversation. You will leave the room.

Do not set boundaries that you don't intend to keep. Show him that you are serious about following up on the consequences that you have stipulated. Don't back down. If you do, this reinforces the message that you are weak and that he does not have to take you seriously.

8. Be ready for changes in your relationship.

When you lay down your personal boundaries, the covert narcissist will see it as a challenge or a threat. He is used to calling the shots. He does not want you to wrest this control from him

He is likely to respond to your boundaries by stepping up on his demands in other areas of the relationship. He might try to punish you by creating emotional distance, giving you the silent treatment, or ignoring you. On the other hand, he may also try to charm or manipulate you so that you give up on the limits you have set. It is up to you to remain steadfast and firm.

How should you behave when you are setting and upholding healthy personal boundaries?

Take this example. Your spouse calls you spiteful, mean, and nasty names. Turn to him, look at him in the eyes, and tell him in a clear, calm, and direct way to stop calling you names. Keep the emotional tone neutral by not showing any emotions.

If your spouse continues to berate you with vile names, leave the room. Put some distance between you and your spouse. Leave the house for a while if you have to. Your refusal to engage shows him that you are not tolerating his behavior. It makes it clear to him that if he insists on behaving in a manner that you have clearly told him you find unacceptable, you will not stand for it.

Call out unacceptable behavior every single time that it happens – not just on occasion. Be consistent so he understands that you are serious about the limits that you have set.

9. Create distance.

Even in healthy relationships, setting new boundaries will result in some discomfort. In emotionally abusive relationships, however, the results can be extremely intimidating, if not downright dangerous.

The covert narcissist may not know how to appropriately respond to your unexpected assertiveness or newfound courage. If the situation becomes highly heated, do not press your point. Your doggedness will not resolve the problem at that moment and may even compromise your safety. Backtrack, at least for the moment. If the same situation happens over and over again, you may need to consider getting in touch with a therapist or a hotline for support and help.

Dealing with a covert narcissist partner, mother, friend, boss, or co-worker leaves you feeling extremely frustrated or overwhelmed.

You have to find means to maintain some healthy distance.

Limit personal interactions. If the covert narcissist is a boss or colleague at work, take breaks on different schedules. Ask to be transferred to a different branch or to another location if possible.

If the narcissist continues to hurt you, cut off contact with him altogether. Keep in mind that the purpose for creating distance is not to upset, pass judgment on, or hurt the other person. It is to protect and keep yourself safe. It is to find the space so you can heal.

Chapter 9
Communication

An emotionally healthy person uses language to communicate with people - to make himself understood, as well as to understand others. A covert narcissist, on the other hand, uses language as a tool to manipulate and control other people. His language usually disguises or hides his true intent.

When two people with no emotional hang-ups chat with each other, they talk WITH each other. When a narcissist joins you in conversation, he talks AT you. He thinks of you as his audience. His self-centered temperament pushes him to dominate the conversation. He talks about things he wants to discuss, sets the manner and mood of the conversation, and converses with an absolute disregard of your interest. He does not hesitate to interrupt you.

A covert narcissist looks meek or modest but he has a subtle way of bringing attention to himself. He has an understated but effective way of invalidating or minimizing what you contribute to the conversation. He sometimes makes it appear that he is listening (if this works in his favor) but the entire purpose of the conversion is self-directed.

Listening to a covert narcissist is not as straightforward as listening to most people. It is more difficult and challenging. You need to see the intent, motivation, thinking, and meaning that underlie what he says (or does not say) so that you are not easily manipulated.

Look at the following phrases that you are likely to hear from a covert narcissist. Then look at the translations – what the narcissist would have said if he were to speak the unvarnished truth.

What he says: "You are being too sensitive."

What he really means: "I don't understand your feelings; I don't even care about them. I want you to listen and understand me but I don't want to do the same for you. If I make you feel guilty or ashamed about your feelings, maybe you will no longer bother me about them."

What he says: "I understand that you are upset but stop blaming me for how you feel!"

What he really means: "Don't make me feel defensive. If something I said or did upset you, you have only yourself to blame for feeling that way. Don't blame me. And don't expect me to accept the blame, apologize, or admit that I am wrong. That will make me look weak. And I am not weak."

What he says: "How did your day go?"

What he really means: "I don't really care. I am just asking so I get to talk about how my day went. I really am not interested about how you are. I am only pretending. What I want to do is to talk about myself and get you to listen with rapt attention and admiration."

What he says: "You are wrong."

What he really means: "I don't really understand or care about what you just said. I just want to plant the seed of self-doubt in you. That will make it easier for me to control and influence you."

What he says: "I have never been surer about anything in my life."

What he really means: "I really am not – and I don't care. I don't care whether what I say is true or even consistent with what I have said before. All I am after is getting what I want. If I speak and act with certainty, you are not likely to question or doubt me. I don't want you to question or undermine me. That is for me to do to you."

What he says: "Stop analyzing what I say and do!"

What he really means: "You make me feel uncomfortable. Don't question my feelings or opinions. I don't care for introspection or doubt. Flatter me. Admire me. Say I am great. Or keep your mouth shut."

What he says: "Hey! That is not what I said at all!"

What he really means: "I may have truly said that but what does it matter? I don't care about how it makes me appear or sound. I think it weakens my image. I will just stonewall you – confuse and exhaust you so that you begin to doubt yourself. It is incredible how easy it is to convince you that you are wrong and I am right just by making it appear that I speak with utmost certainty."

What he says: "How can you say that I don't respect you? I do!"

What he really means: "I don't really; I don't give a darn about you or your rights or needs. I just want your approval, attention, and admiration. I know you admire and hold me in high esteem but what you're doing is not enough for me. I want you to do a better job of it."

What he says: "You keep on saying the same things!"

What he really means: "You probably don't; I don't listen to anything that you say actually. If you want me to change, well, good luck with that. I don't really care how my behavior affects you."

What he says: "You expect too much from me!"

What he really means: "You are not supposed to expect or demand anything from me. Stop complaining. Your role is to see to it that I am happy – to attend to what I need, to give me what I want. Your needs do not count at all."

What he says: "You are being selfish!"

What he really means: "Hey! You are trying to take the spotlight from me! Stop it!"

What he says: "Trust me."

What he really means: "It feels good to say that. I don't really mean it but believe it, nevertheless. Keep on trusting me so I can keep on controlling and using you."

What he says: "Take me for who I am. This is me."

What he really means: "I am not going to change for you. If you challenge me, I will ignore you and make life more miserable for you. See if I care if you leave me. I may try to get you back because I want to continue using you for my self-serving reasons but I actually consider you disposable."

Things to Remember When Talking to a Covert Narcissist

You do yourself a big favor when you do the following things when you are having a conversation with a covert narcissist:

Do not engage. Do not let him provoke you. He will insult you, challenge your confidence, take a jab at your self-worth, or try to demean you. He will do anything to get a rise out of you. Do not insult him back or threaten him. Do not even defend yourself. Stay unengaged.

Talk in a calm, firm, and non-committal manner. When you converse with a covert narcissist, keep in mind that almost all conversations are emotionally loaded. Almost everything that he says has a hidden meaning or self-serving intent behind it. Do not react even if what he says provokes you into wanting to set things right immediately.

Do not say anything out of the strong emotions he may have aggravated. If you are discussing serious matters with him (your children, for example, or logistics about joint property), stick to the points under discussion. Calmly wait for him to respond sensibly. If he continues to criticize, berate, and act in ways that make it impossible for you to discuss the issues in a sensible and productive way, walk away. Tell him you will discuss the matter when he is ready to do so.

Remain unemotional. A covert narcissist will try all means to shake your ability to think and function as a sensible adult. He challenges you in passive aggressive ways. Do not give him the satisfaction of eliciting a heated response from you.

Respond in a straightforward way. Stick to 'yes' or 'no' replies as much as possible. Be simple and factual. "Yes, I will pick the kids up from school at 4 this afternoon." Disregard all his insults or personal stabs.

Pay no attention to his 'love bombs.' A covert narcissist can be quite charming and say lovely things to get what he wants from you. "If you only realize how much I love you." "If you only know how much I want this relationship to work." "I would give anything to make you stay with me."

Do not be naive. Don't take what he says at face value. If you allow yourself to readily believe what he says, you give him the power to suck you right back into his vortex.

Use his technique to get what you want. A covert narcissist wants your adulation, admiration, and approval more than anything else. If you really want something from him, use his own technique on him. Get your way by manipulating him into it. Give him what he needs. Be as charming and persuasive as he usually is.

For example, you need him to drive your son to soccer practice because you have to work overtime. Do not just ask him to do it. Use the approach he usually uses on you. "John requests that you drive him to soccer practice today. You know how he loves to spend time with you. You really are good with him. Spending this extra time with him will make him so happy. Can you take him to practice?"

Do not agree or apologize just to appease him. A covert narcissist expects you to agree with everything that he says. He also has the habit of pointing out your faults, making you feel guilty, and expecting you to apologize for your mistakes or slip ups. He does this to gain the upper emotional hand. He wants to control you. He wants to manipulate you into accommodating what he wants. Do not apologize or agree just to appease him. You end up reinforcing his behavior and giving him more power.

Be non-committal. A covert narcissist expects you to agree with what he says – even if both of you know that he is lying. Keep from agreeing or disagreeing. Remain non-committal. If you agree, you encourage his lies, his arrogant and self-entitled ways, or even his delusions. If you disagree, you run the risk of provoking his annoyance or anger; you may even goad him into acting violently.

Try to keep your responses to a 'medium chill.' Keep things brief, unemotional, and even boring. Psychotherapists suggest that you use the following non-provocative phrases:

"I find that interesting."
"I need time to think about it."
"I will get back to you as soon as I can."
"Okay."
"I see."
"Maybe..."
"I don't think I know enough about it to discuss the topic."
"That seems to make sense."
"I am sorry that you feel the way that you do."
"I think I understand what makes you feel that way."
"I will consider what you just said."
"I will be keeping that in mind."
"Maybe we should discuss that later."

Be firm when you end the conversation. Many people find it difficult to end a conversation with a covert narcissist. Inclined to hog the conversation, a narcissist is hard-put to let you, his 'audience,' go. He will try to get you to stay and talk to him longer. To do this, he will try to make you feel guilty. He may even play the dramatic card and cause a scene.

It is prudent to explain limits or boundaries before you start a conversation with a covert narcissist. Tell him from the beginning that you only have 2 or 3 minutes to spare because you have an appointment to go to. When you give fair warning, you make him understand what to expect. He has no cause to say that you are being discourteous or uncivil to him; you solidify the fact that you feel that it is 'right' to leave.

Know what to expect from a conversation with a covert narcissist. Prepare for it. Set your limits. By doing all these, you reduce his power to make you feel rude, guilty, ill-mannered, blameworthy or worse.

The Gray Rock Technique

Sometimes you have no choice. You have a covert narcissist in your life and it is not an option for you to have nothing to do with him.

Do you have to put up with his emotional abuse? Do you have to endure his hold over you? No. You may have no choice about having him in your life but you certainly have the option of not having him play havoc with your mind.

By using the Gray Rock technique, you CAN put some emotional (and probably promote some physical distance, too) between the covert narcissist and you.

The gray rock is exactly what it is – gray, nondescript, dull, and uninteresting. It generates no excitement, elation, or thrill whatsoever. It is BORING. And because of its lack of any creditable characteristics, people tend to take no notice of it. They ignore it.

The best way to deal with a covert narcissist is to have nothing to do with him, to have no contact in whatever form with him. But there are situations where things are not this simple. Sometimes, you just can't cut the covert narcissist entirely out of your life.

Even if he is your ex, you have children with him. If he is your boss or your colleague, you have to work in the same office with him. If he is a parent, sibling, or friend, you have to see him occasionally at gatherings.

So what do you do?

Consider the nature of a covert narcissist. He wants to manipulate and control you so that you give him what he needs – approval, validation, and admiration. He finds it exhilarating to coerce, stage-manage, and manipulate your thoughts and emotions. He finds that thrilling, challenging, and exciting.

He finds it fun to confuse and bewilder you and make your life chaotic and miserable. He gets his fix from maneuvering things so that you obey, praise, adore him and choose to consider his needs and subjugate yours for them.

If you don't respond to his maneuverings and remain indifferent, untouched, and apathetic, imagine how crushed he feels. When you remain emotionally unresponsive to everything he does – if his bait fails to elicit the response he wants and expects, he is likely to look for a more responsive subject.

A covert narcissist finds your response addictive. If you respond the way he wants you to, he will relentlessly continue to provoke you and find satisfaction in that. If he fails to get what he wants from you, he will look somewhere else for his fix. He will find you boring and useless – as dull, nondescript, and useless as a gray rock.

Being a Gray Rock

So how do you act like a gray rock would?

Keep conversations short and simple. If there is no important reason to talk with him, don't.

Request your office to give you a work area is as far away from him as possible.

When you are separated from him and have to drop your children off at his house, stay in the car.

When having meals at home with a narcissist sibling or parent, stay at the other end of the table.

Keep interactions to a minimum. When you have no recourse but to talk to him, talk about something boring. If he asks questions, keep your answers short and uninspired. Do not prolong the conversation.

When he asks, "How are you doing?" Just say, "I'm okay; thanks." If he asks what you did during the weekend, keep your response non-committal and uninteresting. "I did laundry." If he says, "You're boring," just nod your head. If he asks for your opinion, respond with a vague "Hmmm," "We'll see," or "Maybe." Don't give him the opening to go further into a conversation.

Don't discuss your personal life. Don't hint at how well your life is going. Keep mum about how great you feel. The information will trigger envy and provoke him further into putting you down. Do not suggest in any way, even unintentionally, that your life is somehow better than his. The slightest suggestion to this effect is likely to enrage him.

Do not ask him any question. Don't feel obligated to have "small talk" with him. He is likely to grasp at any opening to engage with you, tell you about his life, and belittle you.

When he talks about a mutual acquaintance, don't react.

Stick to specific information. (To a boss): "We have 8 new clients this month." (To your husband): "The doctor says to give John (your son) acetaminophen for his fever every 6 hours." (To a mother): "Dinner with the Joneses is at 8pm on Thursday."

Stick to topics that the narcissist will find no cause to challenge. You want to avoid getting into a debate or argument with him.

Do not mention the past at all. If he mentions it, be nonchalant about it. Revisiting bad times will just make old issues and hurts resurface. He will find it a good opportunity to play the blame game.

Remain calm and collected, especially when you feel like screaming your head off. Do not flinch. Bite your tongue if you have to.

How the Covert Narcissist is Likely to React to You Turning Gray Rock

The covert narcissist may not understand exactly what it is you are doing but he WILL notice the changes in your behavior towards him.

He is likely to react with anger. This is not new to you, of course, as it is one of the more common strategies a covert narcissist uses to set you off. He may rant, shout, and may even threaten you. Stay cool, unruffled, and self-possessed. Do not react to his anger.

He may also mock and ridicule you for remaining silent or unresponsive. He may call you names, laugh scornfully at you, or deride you in an attempt to draw out an emotional response from you. Stay stoic.

He may also try to use other people (your kids, friends, or colleagues) against you. Sadly, he is not likely to stop short of making up stories about you to draw you into an altercation with him. He may lie to turn people against you and get them to bully you.

He may even threaten you or people close to you. If you think he is making empty threats, hold your ground. If you feel the slightest hint of truth in his threats, get guidance and protection from family, friends, and the authorities (the courts, police, agencies against violence, etc.).

Stay steadfast. If you are able to maintain your non-responsive stance, you will soon note a change in the covert narcissist's behavior. He may not immediately stop pushing your buttons but he is likely to do it less frequently. He is likely to become bored and sick-and-tired of playing the game. Do not take this to mean that he will not attempt to rile you again. He may do so again but as long as you stand your ground, you will be all right.

Do not expect the narcissist to be remorseful. He has very limited ability to realize how much he is hurting you. He is so self-focused that he is unable to sense how you feel. He is not likely to grasp the emotional damage his behavior does to you; neither is he likely to accept responsibility for it.

The Downside to Going Gray Rock

Using the Gray Rock technique may prove effective when you deal with a covert narcissist. However, it also has some risks associated with it.

First, your success may stop you from applying a better technique – that of having no contact with the narcissist. If the option of no contact is open to you, make that your priority.

Cut him from your life if you can. Having unnecessary interactions with him puts you at risk of getting sucked back into your former miserable life. Even if you feel that you have the Gray Rock technique down pat, one small slip-up can make you fall right back into his trap.

Second, without recognizing what you are doing, you may embrace the technique so tightly that you allow it to be your modus operandi in all your relationships. You may form the habit of using the silent treatment, becoming passive and indifferent, and losing passion, interest, and involvement in worthwhile relationships. You may form the habit of numbing yourself to emotions, including empathy, afraid that they leave you vulnerable to being manipulated and controlled by other people.

Take the Gray Rock approach with the covert narcissist. However, learn to be honest and open with other people. Do not put a distance between you and others just because you have had an unhappy relationship with one person. Learn to trust again.

Chapter 10   Seeking Professional Help

When you are in an abusive relationship with a covert narcissist, the abuse can come in many forms.

It can come in the form of financial abuse. The abusive person has total control of your financial resources. You don't have access to money; you are completely dependent on him for your financial and material needs.

It can come in the form of verbal abuse. The abusive person constantly berates, threatens, insults, and yells at you – for no apparent reason at all.

It can come in the form of emotional abuse. The abusive person makes you feel small, guilty, and totally vulnerable.

It can come in the form of sexual abuse like rape.

The abuse can spiral uncontrollably that it may require you to leave the relationship.

Seeking Professional Help

Having a covert narcissist in your life can have serious adverse emotional effects but many people tend to play down the emotional outcome of their abusive relationships.

More often than not, you tell yourself that you are not in extreme emotional pain or that you can handle the struggle on your own. If the emotional abuse continues, however, you may soon find yourself suffering from mental/emotional health symptoms that will interfere badly with your personal happiness or work. It is not wrong to ask for help.

As the old adage says, "Do not wait for the house to fall apart before you fix the windows." Regardless of where you are in your journey towards healing, explore the avenues of help that are available to you. Getting help does not only make the process easier; it is also a form of self-compassion.

Living with a covert narcissist brings a lot of trauma into your life. Even if you decide to leave the narcissist, you still have a lot of emotional issues to sort out. The pain that comes with emotional abuse, whether it is in the past or the present, is so great that it may help to talk to a healthcare professional.

The following indicators may help you decide whether it is the right time to get professional help:

- You worry about your personal safety. You feel that your current living situation undermines your physical safety and you do not know how to resolve the situation.

- You fear the situation that you are in; you see it as volatile and potentially explosive.

- You feel helpless, unable to process your strong and powerful emotions.

- You have recurring bouts of depression.

- You have frequent anxiety attacks.

- You are always afraid.

- You startle easily.

- You have frequent flashbacks and nightmares that make breathing difficult and cause you to sweat profusely.

- You can't sleep.

- You can't eat.

- You are losing weight for no apparent reason at all.

- You find yourself having to use drugs often to help calm you down.

- You find it difficult to manage even simple, routine tasks.

- You don't feel like leaving your bed in the morning.

- You feel useless and worthless.

- Even if you have already left the relationship, you still feel emotionally battered.

A therapist helps facilitate healing if you are dealing with the trauma and emotional issues associated with having a covert narcissist parent. He enables you to recognize the failings of your narcissistic mother (or father). He helps you to acknowledge your childhood pain and its adverse effects. He helps you to break free from the harmful core beliefs that are usually the result of the harmful parenting style you've suffered from. He also helps you substitute a more positive, healthier voice for the negative maternal one that seems to echo in your head. He enables you to heal, restore your self-esteem, regain your emotional balance, and move forward.

It helps to talk to a therapist if your relationship with a covert narcissist partner is giving you sleepless nights and miserable days. If you are dithering between leaving the relationship and giving it another chance, talking to a professional can help you gain perspective. It helps you process your feelings. It helps you sort out your emotions, as well the reasons behind the decision to stay or leave the relationship. It strengthens your resolve to do one or the other. It helps you come up with strategies so that you don't find yourself in a similar situation in the future.

A therapist provides you with options you can use to deal with the anxiety or depression. He helps you overcome predispositions for self-harm and suicide. He enlightens you about whether or not you should tell family and friends about the abuse. When you have left the abusive relationship, he helps you to fight urges to go back to it.

It helps to have someone coach you through the difficult process of understanding and healing. A doctor or therapist can listen attentively to you, evaluate the process, and suggest techniques you can apply to make the process of healing easier.

A therapist helps you move forward. He helps you reflect on your situation, as well as on the underlying personal factors that put you at risk to patterns of abuse. He also suggests ways for you to build your self-esteem and develop new coping skills.

Getting yourself to talk to a therapist is a significant step in your journey towards healing and regaining your emotional wellbeing. Therapy provides you with a safe and nurturing space where a compassionate, well-trained professional helps you look at, understand, and address the volatile emotions that you are struggling with. It helps facilitate healing.

Chapter 11   Leaving an Emotionally Abusive Relationship

It is never easy to leave or end a significant relationship. It is even more difficult to leave a relationship with a covert narcissist – one that finds you cut off from your friends and family, without financial resources, emotionally beaten down, and even in fear of your physical safety.

When circumstances push you to choose whether to leave or stay, you feel terrified, uncertain, torn, and confused. You are scared stiff imagining your partner's anger when he finds out that you want to leave him. You are confused and indecisive; your feelings vacillate between despair and the hope that things will get better. You want to hang on but also desperately want to leave.

You worry about what is going to happen to your partner if you leave him; you feel responsible for him. You may even think that you are somehow to blame for the situation you are in. You are consumed by guilt, fear, self-blame, and confusion.

If you find yourself in an emotionally abusive relationship, keep in mind that it is not your fault that your partner abuses or mistreats you.

You are not to blame for his abusive behavior. You are a good person; you should be treated with respect. You are worthy of having a life that is safe, happy, and meaningful. You deserve to live without fear. You do not have to fight the fight on your own. You are not responsible for your partner's happiness.

What Makes Leaving Difficult?

Other people tend to wonder what makes an individual stay in an unhealthy, emotionally abusive relationship. "Why doesn't she just pack up and leave?" When a person has no experience being in such a relationship, he may indeed find it impossible to understand how the mind of an abused person works.

If you are in an emotionally abusive relationship with a covert narcissist, it is prudent to take some time off to go over the reasons why you find it difficult, almost impossible, to think about making an exit from the relationship.

- You cling to the hope that your partner will change his ways.

A covert narcissist has deep psychological issues. While it is always possible for him to change his ways, he is not likely to. If change does happen, it is not going to be easy or immediate.

He has to want to change. He has to realize that he, and he alone, is responsible for his behavior. He has to acknowledge full responsibility and stop blaming his behavior on his miserable childhood, you, his temper, stress, his drinking, work, or other things outside himself. He also has to seek professional help.

Counselors say that there are certain signs that indicate that a covert narcissist is not likely to change.

He trivializes the abuse. He denies that he is exploiting or manipulating you; he says that you are just imagining or making things up. He accuses YOU of exploiting him. When compelled to face his emotionally cruel behavior, he puts the blame on childhood experiences or on other people, including you.

He makes up stories to get your sympathy and that of your friends or family. He insists that you give him another chance; he makes you feel guilty and forced into the corner. He says that he needs you so he can change.

He refuses to go or to stay in therapy. He agrees to go to counseling in exchange for certain things from you.

- You believe you can help him work through his issues.

The desire to help your partner is natural. However, to believe that you are the only one who can help him, understand him, and help him fix himself is off the mark.

When you stay and accept being repeatedly abused, you enable and reinforce the behavior. You perpetuate the problem. You are not helping your partner.

- Your partner has made a promise to stop emotionally maltreating you.

A covert narcissist can be quite charming just to get his way. When you put your foot down and tell him that you are not allowing him anymore to emotionally manipulate you, he is likely to entreat you to forgive him and to give him the chance to change his ways. He will promise you anything.

He probably means what he says, at least for the moment. His self-serving objective, however, is to get you to stay. When you do, he is likely to immediately go back to his emotionally manipulative ways.

- He agrees to go to counseling.

You may take this as a good sign. However, it should not be the deciding factor for you to stay. You have no guarantee that he will change. In spite of therapy, he may remain abusive and controlling. If you decide not to leave, it should be for the simple unequivocal reason that you love him – and not because you hope that he becomes a better man.

- You worry about the consequences of your leaving the relationship.

The thought of leaving the relationship fills you with a lot of fears. What will your partner do? Where will you go? How will you support yourself? How will you rebuild your self-confidence?

The desire to remain safe (and alive), however, should prompt you to leave as soon as you can. Recognize the fact that you are leaving an unhealthy, as well as a dangerous, situation. That is reason enough to gather your courage and leave. Moreover, there are friends and family, as well as shelters, job training, childcare, legal services, and crisis hotlines available to help you. You are not alone.

Working on an Exit Plan

Some situations make it imperative for the abused person to take steps to leave. Emotional neglect or maltreatment can lead to serious and enduring effects on the psyche. It can also lead to physical violence and abuse.

You should think twice about remaining in the abusive relationship if your partner shows no intention or inclination whatsoever to work on his poor choices or to change his behavior. If you stay, the decision may eventually result in serious repercussions on your physical and emotional wellbeing.

It may help to talk to an astute confidante or a therapist about your options. You may also want to write down the pros and cons of leaving to clear your mind and get rid of lingering doubts about your decision.

You need to be clear and sure about your reasons for wanting to leave. Do not feel coerced to make an immediate decision if you have serious misgivings about what the right thing to do is. Doubts will just make it easy for your partner to use his wiles to suck you back into the relationship. You have to be certain beyond any doubt that leaving is what you want to do – that it is the right thing to do.

Your conviction will enable you to stand your ground.

Don't bother to make empty pronouncements or threats. They will only forewarn your partner and make it more difficult for you to leave. When you threaten to leave in the hope that your threats will make your partner change, you are bound to be immeasurably disappointed. He may resort to 'love bombing' and swamp you with declarations of love and adoration or make grand promises to make you stay. Stay and you will eventually find out that he has no intention to keep his promises.

Once you have considered all angles and have come to the conclusion that leaving is the right option, do so with conviction and without fanfare. Making a quick, quiet exit is the best thing to do.

Keep in mind that nobody deserves to be emotionally abused, threatened, bullied, and made to feel small and worthless. Break free from the covert narcissist and the self-blame, guilt, and loss of your sense of self – and start the process of rebuilding and healing yourself.

Making the Exit

An effective exit plan calls for reflection, discernment, and conviction. It also requires planning and preparation.

Take steps to keep yourself safe.

Your partner can get extremely disturbed, burst out in anger, and even become hostile or violent when he senses that you want to leave him. Take the necessary precautions to protect yourself.

Do not stay in the same room with him if you see his anger build up. Identify areas in the house where it is safe for you to go. Keep away from bathrooms, closets, and small, enclosed rooms with no exits. A room that has a phone and a window or a door that leads outside is your best choice.

Come up with a signal or code that will immediately alert people you trust– neighbors, family, or friends, that you are in danger so they can seek assistance or come to help you right away.

Make arrangements so you can leave when the time is right, even at a moment's notice. Prepare and stash clothing, emergency cash, and important documents and contact numbers in a safe place (for example, in your sister's house). Gas up the car. Keep a spare key within easy reach.

Prepare for a quick and safe exit. Practice if you have to. If you have kids, rehearse the exit plan with them.

Make a list of important emergency contacts, including trusted friends and family, the domestic violence hotline, local shelter, police, etc. Memorize them if you can.

Be prepared. Get in touch with trusted family or friends. Make the necessary arrangements. Who can give you a ride if you don't have a car? Who can give you a temporary place to stay in while you make arrangements for more permanent lodgings? Who can help you contact the police should the need arise?

Consider going to a domestic violence shelter as an option.

You can take temporary refuge in a domestic violence shelter. A shelter seeks to provide the basic living needs of victims of emotional or physical abuse. They also refer you to other organizations that can help you with legal services, financial assistance, support groups, counseling, employment opportunities, services for your children, and other forms of assistance to get you back on your feet.

What to Expect After You Leave

A covert narcissist will not accept your leaving sitting down. It is a big blow to his feeling of self-importance and entitlement. Seeing that his 'love bombing' and charm did not work, he may resort to threats. He may get in touch with your friends and family to demean you. He may stalk you and try to get in touch with you.

Cut off all means of contact. Block his text messages, calls, and emails. If you allow him to get in touch with you, he will just try to reel you back in. If you have children with him, make it a point that you are with a trusted family member or friend when you have to make scheduled custody handovers. Make meetings quick.

Face what has happened to you for what it was. Accept the painful feelings and emotional wounds. Accept them and you will have the strength to move past them and find healing. You will also take back personal power and control over your own life.

Some people feel ashamed or guilty about having been abused. They sometimes minimize the experience and tell themselves that the experience was not really all that bad. Some even try to repress the memory of the experience, hoping that if they don't acknowledge or recognize it, it will simply go away.

Acknowledging the abuse, however, is an essential step for healing. If you keep on ignoring that it has happened, it is likely to create a longer-lasting negative impact in your life. Acknowledge the abuse that you have gone through. It requires great strength to think about the pain but you have to accept the emotional abuse as something that has really happened.

Give yourself time and permission to grieve. Regardless of the extreme emotional difficulties you had during the relationship, expect your breakup to be painful. You will feel confused, angry, sad, and bereft. Let yourself grieve for the shared commitments and dreams that you have lost.

Accept that healing does not come easily or quickly. Seek out friends and family for emotional support. Keep yourself busy and productive so you don't' spend too much time dwelling on your sadness and thoughts of 'what might have been.'

Don't expect your partner to share your feelings of loss. When he finally realizes that you are not coming back to him, he will not spend too much time grieving for losing you. He is likely to immediately look for someone to control and manipulate, to fill his need for admiration. Do not take his shallow feelings personally. They do not reflect on you. They illustrate how one-sided a relationship with a covert narcissist can be.

Take the necessary steps to heal. You will still feel the adverse effects of the relationship long after you break free of it. There will be scars. You will feel the surge of upsetting emotions every now and then. You will have distressing memories. You will have bouts of unreasonable fears that you are in danger. You may also feel disconnected and numb. You may have a hard time learning to trust other people again.

Join support groups. Seek therapy or counseling. Talking about what you have been through will help you process your thoughts and feelings more effectively.

Make friends with yourself. Do not jump at the first opportunity to build a new intimate relationship. Go slow. Spend the time on reflection and get to know yourself better. Engage in activities to build your self-esteem and confidence. Learn from the experience. Take the time to heal.

Chapter 12   Anger and Forgiveness

All stories about emotional abuse in relationships are extremely sad and painful. However, many stories have hopeful endings, suggesting that it is always possible to overcome negative situations. The success of erstwhile victims continues to demonstrate that one can transform himself over time and effectively leave an emotionally abusive situation.

There are also stories that tell of victims who fail to become unstuck from the bonds of an emotionally abusive relationship. Victims remain trapped for a good number of reasons. Some do not have the financial resources to leave the relationship. Some lack a solid support system to help them make the move to break free. Some can't bring their children with them and can't leave them behind either. Victims who find themselves in any of these situations decide that they have no choice but to stay in the relationship, at least for the meantime. There are also stories that narrate how a person tries to justify staying in an abusive relationship that is potentially in her control to change.

Experts in the counseling profession say that a large part of being able to leave an abusive relationship has to do with your decision to look at yourself differently. You are a victim in the relationship but you don't have to remain one your entire life. When you make the effort to rise above your 'I-am-a-victim' pattern of thinking, you open new avenues to make your freedom happen.

The process of getting past the 'victim' mindset includes anger as a defining emotion.

You realize and acknowledge that you are being emotionally abused.

Many victims do not really realize that they are being abused. Some people think that is all right for another person to criticize, demean, humiliate, and make them feel unlovable or unworthy. They somehow feel that they deserve to be treated this way. They feel that they are being punished – not abused. When you feel this way, you don't really see yourself as a victim.

You need to be aware that the relationship you have is an abusive one before you can take steps to break free from the bond. When you start to understand that you are, in fact, being emotionally abused, you take the first significant step.

When you start to recognize that you don't deserve to be treated this way, a shift occurs, in your perspective, as well as in your emotions. You begin to see yourself as a victim, which is what you really are.

You become angry for being emotionally abused.

The realization comes with strong emotions. You get exceedingly upset and disturbed. You start to see your situation as unmerited and unjust – as fundamentally wrong. Some people feel frustrated, aggravated, and hopeless. Others get really angry.

Feeling angry over being emotionally abused is generally a good thing. It acts as a motivating force. Realizing that you are being unjustly maltreated – and getting angry about it, makes you think strongly about your right to do something to make the situation right. Your anger fuels your drive to either correct the situation or, failing that, leave the relationship.

You use your anger to make changes in your situation.

If you are not able to channel your anger properly, it can have adverse, if not dangerous, results. It can lead you to attack the person causing the emotional abuse. It can provoke more aggressive retaliation or physical reprisal. It can result in legal complications. The relationship becomes even more unstable and explosive.

You can also become angry with yourself. You can't stop rebuking yourself for being weak, foolish, and pathetic. You are upset and can't seem to stop berating and beating yourself up. Your anger undermines your self-esteem further. You continue to torture yourself with your self-directed anger.

The best thing that can happen is for you to use that anger to bring on a positive outcome. Use your anger to motivate you to take action to leave the relationship – something that usually really needs to be done.

You let go of your anger.

You acknowledged that you were a victim of abuse. You faced the strong emotions that came with the realization. You used your anger to give you the wit and boldness to leave your relationship.

Once you have become free of the relationship, there is no longer any need for your anger. It is time to let it go.

Stop feeling angry with yourself for allowing yourself to stay so long in the relationship. Forgive yourself. Stop picking at your emotional scars. You have managed to get yourself out; that is something to rejoice in and feel good about.

Try to gain a forgiving perspective about the person who has abused you, too. Think of him as a person who is battling his own psychological demons. Remaining angry with him will not do you any good.

It will be difficult for you to erase the hurtful memories. If you can't move on, though, you allow yourself to remain in the past. It would have been as if you had not managed to escape from the emotionally abusive relationship at all.

Remind yourself that "to live well is the best retribution." Be forgiving. Your anger does not serve any good purpose now. Let it go and get on with your new life.

Letting Go of Bitterness and Hate

It is difficult to let go of the bitterness and hurts that result from being in an emotionally abusive relationship – even after you've left the relationship. You tend to hold on to the resentment, bitterness, and anger. You sometimes even entertain thoughts of taking revenge on the person that hurt you.

The covert narcissist, the person who abused you, is usually someone close to you, someone you care about. It can be your partner, your mother, a friend, or a colleague. The abusive relationship can cause many deep emotional scars. Even after you have left the relationship, just thinking about the person and what you have gone through can be emotionally exhausting. You wonder whether it is possible to recover from the experience. It seems almost impossible to pull through and move forward with your life.

When you are hurt, especially by someone you trust and care about, you feel confused, sad, and angry. If you continue thinking about the hurt, the resentment and desire for revenge can take root. You choose to forget about whatever positive feelings you have about the experience and wallow in the negative feelings instead. You can't let go of your grudges. You stagger under a heavy and bitter sense of injustice.

There are individuals who find it easy to forgive; and there are those who find it almost impossible to do so. Healthcare professionals say that a victim of emotional abuse must learn to forgive – if only for his own good.

Holding grudges has several adverse effects. You carry the bitterness and anger over to new experiences and other relationships. You find it hard to enjoy the present because you are wrapped up in the bitter past. You become anxious or depressed and find it hard to find meaning and purpose in life.

The bitterness undermines your spiritual beliefs. The anger and resentment chip away at your connectedness to other people. You become suspicious of people. You become wary and afraid to trust. Because of this fear, you turn your back on opportunities to develop enriching and valuable relationships with other people.

For your physical and emotional wellbeing, you have to let go of your grudges and learn to forgive.

Learning to Forgive

Being able to forgive is essential to healing. If you do not learn to forgive, you continue the pattern of hurt. You continue to feel the pain. Therapists who help patient regain their emotional health and balance say that forgiveness promotes healing. It leads to hope, joy, and peace. It brings wellbeing; it nurtures physical, emotional, and spiritual health.

What is forgiveness?

People view forgiveness in different ways. Forgiveness generally refers to letting go of resentments and thoughts of retribution.

You may still remember the hurt and the offense – they may remain with you for a long time, but when you forgive, the emotional damage reduces its grip on you. By forgiving the person who has hurt you, you diminish his control over you. You start to break free from the psychological control he has over you. By forgiving him, you even open the possibility of understanding him and feeling compassion for him.

To forgive does not mean to forget or to justify the harm. It does not require that you make up with the person responsible for hurting you. It simply means that you allow yourself to let go of the feelings of pain and resentment. Forgiveness results in the inner peace that enables you to go on with your life.

To forgive is to decide to commit to a personal process of change. It is a decision to move from pain to absolution.

Open your eyes to the benefits of forgiveness and what healing can do to make your life better. Forgiving the covert narcissist is good for your physical health. You lower your blood pressure. You strengthen your immune system. You improve your heart health.

You also enjoy emotional benefits from choosing to forgive. When you let go of rancor and bitterness, you open the way for improving your self-esteem. You experience less stress and anxiety. As you let go of feelings of hostility, you improve your mental health. You reduce the risk of depression. You enjoy healthier relationships.

Take the time to recognize the areas that require healing. What are the emotions associated with the pain that you have gone through? How do these emotions affect your behavior? What are the positive ways for you to release these emotions?

Think about the person who has hurt you and the need to forgive him. Make a conscious decision to forgive him. When you do, you cut off the power and control that person wields over you. You take responsibility for the process of healing.

As you let go of your grudges, you realize that the hurtful experience does not define you or your life. You start to feel free. You are able to let go of the anger and move on towards a better life.

It is difficult to forgive. If you feel stuck, try to see the relationship from the other person's point of view. What pushed him to behave the way he did? Were his behaviors provoked by emotional hurts? Were they prompted by some psychological weaknesses? Think of the times you have hurt others. Think about the people who have forgiven you. Try to grow in self-insight and understanding. Pray, meditate, or express your feelings by writing on a personal journal.

Recognize that forgiveness is a gradual process. You sometimes feel the need to revisit small hurts. You feel the resentment wash over you again. You need to forgive over and over again.

Accept the fact that forgiveness does not always lead to reconciliation – and that this is okay. In some case reconciliation is not appropriate. However, even if reconciliation is not possible, forgiveness always is. It is a choice that you make.

If you find it hard to go through the healing process on your own, look for a person who can give you counsel -- someone who has wisdom and compassion, like a spiritual leader or an impartial friend. You may also want to consider the possibility of seeking the help of a professional emotional health care provider or joining support groups.

Look at forgiveness in terms of the peace, joy, and emotional and spiritual healing it brings you. Forgiveness does not mean that the

135

person you forgive will change his behavior. That is beyond your control. What is within your control is learning to forgive – and enjoying the liberating and healing sense of peace that comes with it.

Chapter 13   Practicing Self-Care

There are a number of simple and practical self-care practices to help you tend to your body, mind, and spirit after suffering from emotional abuse.

You may find some of the suggestions simple or seemingly trivial. Keep in mind that being in a relationship with a covert narcissist will sometimes make you feel so hopeless that you fail to give yourself the self-care that you need.

Self-care is essential to your healing process. When you take the time and effort to take care of your needs, you are telling yourself that you are a person of worth. You deserve to be healthy in body and mind. By giving your needs the attention they deserve, you also get the nutrients, support, and energy to prevail over the emotional difficulties that you face.

Here are some practical tips to start you on your journey to heal and regain control over your life:

1. Eat right.

Eating right is a significant component of the ability to heal from emotional abuse. It has

137

powerful effects on your physical, mental, and emotional wellbeing.

When you are in a volatile relationship, you go through intense emotions and pain that make it difficult for you to eat properly. You either lose the appetite to eat or you turn to food for comfort and binge on the wrong food like salty, fatty, and sugary food. When you don't eat enough or make the wrong food choices, your body finds it hard to regulate not only your energy levels but your emotions, as well. It makes healing difficult.

Eat sensibly. Do not skip meals. Include fruits and vegetables in your diet. Eat protein-rich food. Drink a lot of water. Eat less processed food or fast food.

These rules may be simple but they go a long way into nourishing your body and enhancing mood. You have more energy. You feel less tired and despondent. You can concentrate better. Moreover, when you go out of your way to nourish your body, you are sending a positive message to yourself. You are reinforcing the message that you are valuable and that you deserve to be taken care of.

2. Exercise.

Don't play down the advantages of physical exercise.

Try to get some exercise done in the morning. It infuses you with energy and gets the blood going. Exercise helps the body to produce and release norepinephrine, dopamine, and serotonin, natural brain chemicals that trigger feel-good sensations.

Exercise helps to buffer the ill-effects of stress, anxiety, and depression. It promotes a sense of wellbeing. Just a few minutes of morning exercise will help chase off negativity and brighten your mood.

There are several ways to get a few minutes of exercise into your day. You can go for a run or a brisk walk around the block. You can go to the local gym. You can also opt to do some helpful exercises like yoga or stretching at home.

3. Get enough sleep.

Sleeping well at night is one of the keys to health and wellbeing. It strengthens your immune system. It improves mood and memory. It allows you to concentrate and be productive. It makes you feel good. Not getting enough sleep, on the other hand, makes it hard to maintain a positive disposition. You always feel irritable, exhausted, and worn out.

The following are indications of sleeping poorly:

You feel sleepy and short-tempered during the day.
You fall asleep while driving.
You can't concentrate on what you are doing.
People always tell you that you look sick or washed-out.
Your reactions are slow.
You can't control your emotions.
You feel like you need a nap all the time.
You need caffeine to keep you awake.

Going through an emotionally abusive relationship makes it hard to get enough sleep. The emotional stress and anxiety that the trauma causes tend to keep you on edge and awake. You find it hard to fall asleep and stay asleep. You lie awake at night feeling angry, anxious, and miserable. If you do manage to fall asleep, it is a restless kind of sleep. You oftentimes wake up too early and still feel tired and fretful. All you want to do is crawl back to bed – even if you know that you will just lie there, awake and unable to get the rest that you need.

Emotional trauma keeps you in a cycle of anxiety and sleep deprivation. You feel anxious so you can't sleep. You don't get enough sleep so you feel more anxious. The cycle plays havoc with your already somewhat wobbly physical, emotional, and mental functioning.

Try to get the sleep that you need by addressing the two-pronged problem. Find ways to reduce the anxiety and to induce sleep.

Reducing Stress

To help you sleep, use the following techniques for reducing stress:

Meditate. Take your mind off your problems by focusing on your breath. Inhale slowly and deeply. Let the breath out just as slowly.

Do some physical exercises during the day. Exercise serves as an effective outlet for negative feelings. Consider doing yoga. It relieves stress. It makes you feel better.

Play soft and soothing music. It reduces blood pressure. It calms the mind and relaxes the body.

Use anxious energy in productive ways. Help a neighbor. Do volunteer work. Making life easier for other people takes your mind off your own problems.

Talk to a person you trust. Seeing a therapist or talking to a friend helps ease your worries.

Inducing Sleep

You will find it easier to sleep if you follow certain routines.

Make sleep a priority. Block out 7 to 8 hours for sleep. It helps to go to bed and arise at the same time each day – even on weekends.

Do not take nicotine, chocolate, coffee, or other similar stimulants before going to bed. Do not use the computer, watch TV, pay bills or engage in any activity that is likely to stimulate the mind. Instead, do something calming like meditation or listening to mood music.

Make your surroundings conducive to sleep. Dim the light. See to it that the bedroom is cool and quiet. Use pillows and a mattress that are comfortable.

Associate the bedroom with sleep. Use the bed only to sleep on. Do not watch TV or do your work in your bedroom. Lie down only when you are ready to sleep. If you can't fall asleep within 20 minutes, do something soothing or relaxing in another room.

Exercise but do not do so close to sleeping hours. It is better to work out in the morning or afternoon so you don't get too stimulated or energized close to sleeping hours.

Stop checking the time. It will only make you more anxious.

If your sleeping problems become so severe that they start to undermine your health, see a doctor.

4. Make your bed as soon as you wake up.

A lot of people look at this particular suggestion as much too simple and probably even silly. However, it really does help set the mood for the rest of the day.

Getting this small task done first thing in the morning triggers a sense of accomplishment that sets the right tone for the day. It makes you feel good about yourself. It tells you that you can get things done and motivates you to do more. It also reminds you that the small things in life matter – that even the little things can be a source of pleasure and satisfaction. Research even indicates that people who make it a habit to make their beds when they arise tend to be more positive in their ways while those who don't do it tend to be moody, timid, and aimless in their ways.

5. See the day as a new beginning.

Thinking about the past can weigh you down. Always keep in mind that today does not have to be as bad as yesterday.

Today is filled with possibilities. It gives you a chance to start anew. It offers the opportunity to shake off the negativity associated with your past and move forward.

Take a few moments to speak out a series of positive affirmations so that you feel hopeful and confident to start your day. Begin the day in the right frame of mind with the following positive morning affirmations:

"I am enough. I will always be enough."
"I can make smart decisions by myself."
"I am letting go of all feelings of self-inadequacy."
"I open myself to everything good that is coming my way today."
"I have courage."
"I am facing my fears."
"I am taking action to make my situation better."

You will learn more about the value of positive affirmations in the next chapter.

6. Keep your day manageable.

Being in an emotionally abusive relationship tends to trigger a load of negative thoughts and feelings that can be quite overwhelming. Some people who are in a similar situation try to flee from being devastated by the negativity by losing themselves in doing things – a lot of things.

Frantically tearing around to accomplish tasks is not the way to constructively deal with negativity. You are just setting yourself up to feel more stress in your life. Rushing around, doing things at breakneck speed, trying to do everything and feeling agitated all day will not make you feel less anxious.

Try to do things in a gentle and measured pace. Keep your tasks for the day at a manageable level and you have a better chance of feeling calm and more peaceful.

Keep your daily routine simple, uncomplicated, and manageable. Set out to do one task at a time; do not multi-task. Control all distractions. Set a schedule for checking emails and messages so that you don't get distracted every single time that you receive a notification. By keeping your routine simple and uncomplicated, you make your life less anxious and exasperating. You minimize stress. You set yourself up to become more effective. You are more likely to be in a better mood.

7. Embrace and be in sync with your desires and needs.

When you are in a relationship with a covert narcissist, you get used to thinking that your only purpose is to cater to what he needs and desires. You stop looking at your own self as someone of value. You forget your own passions, dislikes, interests, etc.

To achieve healing, you need to get in touch with the person you used to be before the relationship, as well as the person you now want to become.

Rediscover who you are. Take time off to be with yourself to think and reflect. What are your dreams and aspirations? What hopes do you want to pursue? What activities kindle your passions?

You don't have to go big right away. Start small. If you have allowed your relationship to stifle your creative and artistic nature, it is probably time to take some painting or pottery lessons. If you have always been interested in sports, take swimming classes or join a bowling team. Do something that you have always been interested in. Treat yourself like you would a person who is important and of great value. Do this and you will regain your sense of self-worth.

Chapter 14   Cultivating the Right Attitude

Being in an abusive relationship with a covert narcissist - or recovering from one – is not easy. It can lead to feelings of hopelessness, defeat, and self-pity. But if you really want to pull yourself out of the mire of these defeatist emotions, YOU CAN.

Use the recommendations outlined in the previous chapters and you are on your way to healing and recovering (slowly and gradually for many individuals – but this is okay; a small step towards healing is something to ALWAYS rejoice about and to take inspiration from).

Mental healthcare professionals also say that having the right attitude helps you make significant strides towards healing.

Many things are not in your control. When you go over the things that you can do to make your life better, you often find yourself constrained by the fact that you have pretty limited options. What is within your control, however, is your attitude. And your attitude is a significant factor in influencing how you live your life.

Attitude refers to the disposition, manner, position, or feeling that a person assumes towards a particular situation, person or thing.

It is an orientation, posture, or tendency, especially of the mind, that the person adopts.

Therapists say that adopting an open, constructive attitude enables victims of emotional abuse to make significant changes in their lives and their relationships.

Be intentional about the demeanor that you assume towards your situation. Accept that it is a tough, painful position to find yourself in but do not allow this to dampen your belief that you can surmount it, that things will get better, and that you will recover from all the pain.

Being mindful about the attitude you choose moves you closer to healing and recovery. It makes you more resilient. It helps you make better decisions. It gets your creative juices flowing. If you choose to look at your situation from a more hopeful perspective, you take big steps from being your unhappy, grouchy, or sullen self to becoming a happy and confident person.

Certain routines or habits help you adopt and maintain a constructive attitude.

Start your day with a put-you-in-a good-mood morning routine.

You have no control over everything that today brings but you definitely have a say on how the day begins.

Find a morning routine that works for you. It should be one that helps to start you off on the right foot. It gives you space to feel hope; it creates a sense of positive anticipation that today will be better than yesterday. It prepares you emotionally and physically to face what the day has in store for you.

Each person has the option to choose a morning approach that works well for him. Some individuals prefer to take to the ground running. Others opt to ease into the day more slowly and gently.

Like everything in life, there is no one-size-fits-all morning routine. Look for a morning routine that fits you like the proverbial glove.

If you thrive on bursts of energy, see to it that you start your morning with something that gives you a strong, powerful push. Go for a morning hike or jog. If you find comfort in planning out everything, set aside time to plan how the day should unfold for you. Create a plan.

If you thrive on mental stimulation, read, write on your journal, or strategize. If you wake up agitated and want to still your racing mind, try meditation.

Look for a morning routine that resonates with you. The routine may take an hour or just 10 minutes. If it works for you – makes you feel energized or grounded, choose that routine.

Choose to be positive.

It may be a little difficult for you have positive thoughts after the emotional trauma you've gone through but you can always try. When you decide to wait for something outside you to kindle positivity, you might wait your entire life.

Try to think of something positive first. Expect something good to happen. You will be surprised by how this change in your outlook sets the tone for your emotions. When you think positive thoughts, your attitude tends to follow suit; it becomes positive, too. When your thoughts are negative, they tend to lead you to developing a similarly negative attitude.

Hit the 'pause' button when you notice that you are having negative thoughts. Think of something positive instead. Do this and you will discover a change in your attitude. You feel lighter, and yes, more positive. Keep in mind that positivity is a choice; it is an attitude that you nurture. It is not a situation.

Smile.

Studies show that the mere act of smiling can give you an immediate boost in attitude. Arrange your facial muscles in a smile while trying to recall a happy memory. This small act sets the stage for the body to release the feel-good hormones serotonin and endorphins. When your body releases natural chemicals favorable to wellbeing, you will find it so much easier to take on a positive attitude.

Fill the brain with positivity.

Thinking about what you have gone through will naturally make you feel unsettled, sad, or angry. In spite of the odds, however, there are a number of things you can do to fill your brain with positivity. Listen to music that uplifts you with its melody or lyrics. Read books or articles that have helpful positive messages. Watch inspiring movies. Find a hobby that enriches the mind and spirit. When you load your brain with positivity, you will find it easier to change your outlook for the better.

Focus on what is good.

Keeping your sight on what is good promotes a positive attitude. When you choose to see the good in yourself, in other people, and in your life, it becomes easier to adopt a positive outlook.

Remain enthusiastic. Life has a way of making you feel exhausted, beat, and bushed. When you have a difficult time maintaining a positive attitude, think of the things that stimulate your interest and enthusiasm and start doing them. Taking action will soon make you realize that you are lucky to be alive.

Seek out people who have a positive outlook.

Positivity is contagious. When you feel down and in need of a mindset boost, seek out somebody who has an incredibly positive outlook in life and find a reason to spend time with him. His attitude will rub off on you and soon you will be able to look at life with renewed hopefulness.

Use the visualization technique.

See in your mind the things that you want to happen *really* happening. This technique allows you to sustain a positive outlook.

During his incarceration, Nelson Mandela found himself in a particularly difficult situation. Things (other than being locked up in a tiny cell that measured barely 6 feet wide) weighed heavily on his mind. His future seemed hopeless. Mandela managed to keep his hopes up by using the visualization technique. He visualized himself walking free. Again and again, he fantasized about being set free and finally being able to do what he wanted to do. Running the wonderful images over and over again in his mind allowed him to keep a positive outlook even when the circumstances he found himself in were really bad.

How things turn out is not exactly within your control. However, by visualizing the outcome you want to see, you refocus your mind on what is positive. You stave off hopelessness. You give yourself a sense of what you want to happen actually happening.

Imagine yourself getting rid of all the hurts and painful feelings you still harbor from the emotionally abusive relationship. See yourself feeling happy, liberated from all the emotional baggage. You are able to trust again. You are building healthy and meaningful relationships.

Run these positive images in your mind several times a day. Visualization helps you to maintain focus about getting a positive outcome.

Be grateful.

After having gone through an emotionally abusive relationship, you tend to focus on the negative – on the things that have gone wrong, on what you are missing out on or have lost, and on the challenges and difficulties that you have to cope with. Get out from the downward spiral that such negativity can bring about.

Make the shift to a positive outlook by being grateful.

Run through your mind the things that you are grateful for and you immediately notice your mood lifting. You start to feel better.

The attitude of gratitude is thinking and feeling; it is both action and mood.

Actively call to mind the many things that you are thankful for. You will notice that as you think about these things, you start to feel happy about them. The thoughts stir up emotions of joy and contentment. You go from thinking about what you are grateful for to feeling good about them. And as the thoughts continue to stir up stronger feelings of gratefulness, your emotions, in turn, tend to bring to mind other things to be grateful for. You get caught up in a positive thought-loop that helps increase both your physical and mental-emotional health.

Start your day with gratitude. Take a moment to bring to mind the things that are working well for you. As you continue to dwell on those things, focus on the swell of appreciation that seems to rise within you. Stay in the moment. Be mindful about how good you feel that you are here. Think about how wonderful it is to receive the gift of this day and its many possibilities.

Learn to appreciate small pleasures.

Even people who lead relatively happy and uneventful lives (i.e., no big emotional traumas) find that big pleasures like weddings, graduations, promotions, having your memoirs published – do not come frequently.

Learn to look for and savor the small victories and pleasures that life gives you. When you are able to nurture the ability to enjoy the small pleasures, simple things like having a bowl of ice-cream, watching the sunrise, or walking barefoot in the park can spark joy.

Research demonstrates that the mere effort of being grateful can have enormous positive results. It enhances your health. It makes you more positive in outlook. It improves your relationships. It makes you more productive. It changes how you look at your life.

Cultivate a Zen attitude.

Taking a Zen approach simply means being mindfully aware of the present moment. You see your experiences as something that happens 'for' you instead of 'to' you.

When remembering what you've been through triggers negative thoughts and emotions, choose to adopt a Zen approach. Stop asking why you went through the emotional abuse or why you are having deep, unhappy feelings about your experience. Instead, try to ask what you are supposed to gain or learn from the experience. How will the experience and your present emotions help you grow and become a more enlightened and better person?

Regular meditation helps you to develop the Zen outlook. It creates a peaceful and contented mind. It increases confidence and self-esteem. It enhances focus.

Meditation is particularly helpful for those who have gone through the torment of having been in an emotionally abusive relationship. It quiets the mind. It helps you manage the anguish and despondence brought about by the insistent surfacing of bad memories.

If you are not used to meditation, start with a quick three or five-minute practice. As you start to feel the benefits of the practice, you may want to progress to lengthier sessions.

Find a quiet place and be seated in a comfortable position. Focus on the moment. Do this by focusing on your breath; inhale and exhale with mindfulness. Relax your body. Empty the mind of everything except its attention on the breath. By turning full awareness onto your breath, you will soon notice a soft and gentle calmness descend over your mind and body. Be present in the moment while you look at yourself with a compassionate and accepting attitude.

The Zen approach helps you to rise above anger, anxiety, frustration, and other negative emotions. It makes you feel more in control. It moves you to respond in a more positive and balanced manner. It helps you acknowledge your emotions, let go of the things that are beyond your control, and learn from your experiences. It helps you maintain a positive perspective.

Take responsibility.

You can choose to remain a victim - or you can choose to be your own 'creator.' Shifting the mode from victim to creator is to assume responsibility for your life. Take charge of your life; pronounce that you are the 'master of your fate.'

You are in charge. You create your life. You are responsible for 'you.' Taking responsibility can feel quite liberating.

Be proactive. You are reacting when you allow circumstances and people to determine how you feel. On the other hand, you are being proactive, when you decide how you should feel regardless of the situation. You choose what to

think and feel. You choose your attitude –
without regard for what the day brings.

Find a purpose. A purpose gives you a fixed
point to think about and to focus on. It keeps
you steady, regardless of the many challenges
you face. Having purpose and meaning in life
does wonders for your outlook.

Do not expect life to be easy.

Life can get really tough – for everyone. It can
be sad and even painful. However, when you
are resourceful and brave, you can take
whatever hardship life dishes out. Face the fact
that life can be hard, believe that you can take
it -- then see how that awareness changes your
attitude for the better.

Stop whining. Complaining or grumbling about
your situation does not help you keep a
constructive outlook. When you complain or
whine, you simply keep on thinking negative
things about your situation or about a person.
You are not resolving your situation. You are
not making things better.

When you complain, you foster negativity.
Instead of focusing on the negative, it is more
prudent (and more fruitful) to start thinking
about what you can do to solve or improve your
situation.

Don't feel entitled. Don't expect good things to be handed to you on a silver platter. When you don't get what you expect, fight the tendency to feel outraged or to blame others for your disappointment.

Work hard so that you increase the chance that you get what you want. Encourage yourself to persist in what you do in spite of initial difficulties. Teach yourself to adapt to change. When you depend on yourself to make things happen, they are more likely to happen. At the very least, you get the satisfaction of knowing that you tried everything to make what you want come about.

Tap your sense of humor. Look at life as funny, as absurd. Try to laugh at your situation. Look at it with a sense of humor. You may need some time to be able to do this but being able to see your situation with a sense of humor helps you regain emotional stability. It lifts your mood and emotions.

Be curious. One of the best ways to approach a 'bad' situation is to think of it as a learning experience. Being curious gives you a present-moment point of reference. It makes you acknowledge your emotions and the uncertainties that you face – and realize that you can survive them. You are able to look at your experience more deeply and generate helpful insights about the experience.

Look for ways to be creative and productive.

Victims of emotional abuse tend to go back again and again to unhappy memories of their relationship. And they feel all the awful emotions yet again.

How do you break away from the powerful pull of painful memories?

Experts say that healing depends on your ability to rewire your brain so that it thinks differently. One way to achieve the thought shift is by focusing on other things. Distract the brain and keep it focused elsewhere.

An effective and productive way to do this is to look for complex, creative, and engaging activities that call for a certain degree of skill and concentration. Learn how to knit, embroider, or do creative stitching. Learn carpentry, pottery, or cake decorating. Take classes in painting or dance. Play a musical instrument. Do gardening.

When you create or tend things by hand, the activity promotes psychological health and wellbeing. It makes you happy.

Taking up a creative hobby keeps you engaged and productive. You lose track of time. You go through something that experts liken to the loss of self. Your mind shifts from dwelling on the miserable past to focus on the now.

The shift happens steadily, without you having to exert a great deal of effort. By doing creative, complex, and repetitive actions, you set your brain in motion. You lead it into focusing its energy on the creative act. The shift in your thought processes helps the brain to build new neural pathways that have nothing to do with past hurtful memories.

Research shows that making the shift is more effective when you do the activity with other people. When you spend time with people who share your interests, you enjoy a camaraderie that is uplifting and soothing. Instead of feeling weighed down by intrusive and muddled memories of a hurtful past, you are able to relax and feel productive. You are able to slowly regain your sense of self.

The act of creating something with your hands keeps your body and mind active. It helps you find your healing place. It helps you to move forward.

Guard against negative self-talk.

'Self-talk' refers to the little voice in your head that feeds you messages all day long. This voice plays a significant role in your self-image, in how you think and feel about yourself.

The messages that this voice repeats over and over again in your head are not always your own. They often echo the messages that you hear from your parents, partner, siblings, friends, colleagues, and other significant individuals in your life.

When you have a covert narcissist in your life, the messages that you hear from him are often mean, negative, discouraging, hurtful, and belittling. When you internalize these messages – when they become part of your self-talk, they undermine your self-esteem. They weaken your sense of self-worth. They take their toll on your ability to trust in yourself. They make it difficult for you to be happy.

Here are some examples of these messages:

"I don't like myself."
"I can't do anything right."
"I can never succeed."
"I do not deserve to be loved."
"I am weak."
"I am stupid."
"I do not deserve to seek things that interest and fulfill me."
"I don't deserve to be happy."
"I screw up all my relationships."
"Everything that is going wrong in my life is my fault."

"I deserve to be miserable."

A covert narcissist manipulates your feelings to isolate you and to push you to cut off your relationships with other people. He says things designed to make you doubt and distrust even the people you love. In time, without you being consciously aware of it, you learn to internalize these messages in your self-talk.

"No one wants to hear about my problems."
"No one wants to help or support me."
"There is no one I can trust."

As you repeat these messages over and over to yourself, you start to believe them and allow them to further influence your thoughts, emotions, and actions.
The messages reinforce feelings of distrust and silent anger - emotions that you probably also feel towards the covert narcissist. They also further undermine your self-esteem.

If you allow these feelings to persist, you run the risk of facing other problems. You develop a critical attitude towards people. You hesitate to communicate your feelings. You are indecisive about approaching even friends and family for help. You feel isolated and start to withdraw from social interactions.

Let go of the harsh and disapproving voice in your head and replace it with a more positive and constructive inner dialogue. A more helpful commentary will make you feel valuable, confident, and worthy of respect. It increases your self-esteem. It helps you grow in self-acceptance. It empowers you to set healthy boundaries, stand up and advocate for yourself, and find peace, joy, and meaning in your life.

Use positive affirmations.

It is not easy to heal from the emotional abuse of being in a relationship with a covert narcissist. But there are certain techniques that can make healing go faster. Using daily affirmations is one of them.

Emotional abuse undermines your self-esteem. It makes you feel unloved, inadequate, and hopeless. You feel that you are never good enough, that you are worthless.

Using daily positive affirmations helps you counter these feelings. It enables you to make an effective shift from feeling worthless to feeling empowered.

By creating a positive internal monologue with affirmations, you help yourself overcome the damaging effects of the emotional abuse. You enable yourself to be less influenced by the harm inflicted by the relationship; you become more resilient to the hurt and pain. You are able to rebuild and reinforce a healthy and stronger sense of self.

The following are examples of these positive affirmations and why they are effective for regaining your sense of balance and self-esteem.

1. "I am taking slow but certain steps, day by day, towards recovery."

This statement serves as a helpful reminder that the healing process takes time. It is not easy to come to terms with having been in an abusive, destructive relationship. You cannot rush the mending. Some people take months, years, or even a lifetime to heal.

This affirmation accepts that reality. It is okay to heal slowly. It is okay to backslide every now and then. It is okay to encounter setbacks. The important thing is to stay on the journey. Taking the journey towards healing is never a waste of time.

Other affirmations that reinforce the same feelings include the following:

- "I am healing slowly but surely from my hurtful relationship."
- "Every single day, I am rebuilding my life and making it more meaningful."
- "I feel certain that healing is possible."

- "I am learning to trust others again."
- "I am learning to break the cycle of thinking and feeling that makes me experience pain again."

2. "I am putting the past behind me."

This affirmation expresses your commitment to have a forward-looking attitude.

It is natural to find your mind drifting towards what has happened. Take the reins and turn it back to the present. When memories associated with the emotional trauma persist, repeat your affirmation to put the past behind. Remain aware of the negative effects of clinging to unhappy recollections. Practice persistence. When you find yourself slipping, forgive yourself but regain control of your thoughts. Letting yourself dwell on the past acts like a chain around you; it keeps you from moving forward.

Here are similar affirmations you may want to use:

- "I am using my energy for the present and future."
- "I am happy to let go of the pain and hurt."
- "I am making peace with what has happened to me."

3. "I deserve to be loved and respected."

A covert narcissist is basically unable to give sincere and genuine affection, care, and respect. Because you have been in a relationship with a person who makes it a point to withhold the respect and love that you need, it is highly possible for you to forget what being treated with affection, consideration, and true kindness feels like.

The affirmation serves as a reminder that you are loveable and should be treated with the respect and concern that every individual deserves.

Other similar affirmations include:

- "I am worthy."
- "I am loveable."
- "I deserve respect."
- "I deserve to have others treat me with kindness."
- "I am a person of value."
- "I am happy to receive love and compassion from others."
- "I allow myself to accept loving thoughts, respect, and praise from others."

4. "I am not to blame for what has happened."

A covert narcissist always puts the blame on you. Everything is your fault. Because of the repetitions of this particular message, you learn to see yourself as guilty. You begin to see yourself as fully responsible for all negativity of the relationship. You feel the intense hurt, guilt, and shame that come from the sense of accountability. You feel disgraced and mortified.

This affirmation helps you see that you are blameless. It helps you rise above the feelings of humiliation and shame. It makes you realize that you are just a victim and that you have nothing to be ashamed of.

Other similar affirmations include:

- "I release all feelings of guilt and shame."
- "I release the inclination to feel accountable."
- "I do not blame myself for the pain and hurt."

5. "It is okay not to be okay."

There will be many moments when you feel frustrated, angry, hurt, gloomy, wounded, or even vengeful. It is prudent to realize that it is all right to feel these emotions. Even people who are in loving relationships can have these feelings.

You have been in a traumatic relationship; it is right that you feel all the emotions of pain, frustration, and anger. Validate these feelings and believe that, in time, you will be able to leave them behind.

This affirmation tells you that it is okay to have these emotions.

Other similar affirmations include:

- "I accept my emotions as part of my journey towards healing."
- "It is all right for me to feel this way. I know that I will be able to recover eventually."
- "I see my emotions as legitimate; I accept them and know that this acceptance will help me heal."

6. "I am responsible for my healing."

Living with a covert narcissist teaches you to hand over control to someone else. This affirmation allows you to take back that control. It reminds you that healing is possible – and that you can make it happen.

Similar affirmations include the following:

- "I choose to surround myself with a sense of security and peace."
- "I choose to love myself."
- "I choose to put my health and wellbeing first."
- "I have the ability to make sound decisions and healthy choices for myself."
- "I choose not to let my experience defeat me."
- "I am able to turn hurtful experiences into something helpful and positive."

Always be careful with the words that you use. Use positive words, even when you are 'talking' to yourself. Research shows that when you use positive self-talk, you bring about helpful results.

Positive self-talk psyches you up. It rouses your willpower. You shift from a can't-do mode to a can-do disposition. You stop worrying that you can't do something and start feeling confident that you can make things happen. You go from doubting success to happily anticipating it, even when the situation is worrying or frustrating.

Conclusion

Thank you for reading this book.

I hope that you now have a clearer understanding of your relationship with the covert narcissist in your life. I hope that you now recognize that all the pain and anguish that you are going through are not your fault – that you are a victim.

I also hope that you now also realize that you can find your way out of the swamp of emotional ache and hurt that characterizes your relationship – that you are now ready to use the tips and techniques outlined in the book to reclaim your life.

It is not easy to heal from emotional trauma. It is a journey characterized by pain, struggle, and imperfections. You will often waver and falter in your efforts. There are times when you just want to give up. When you realize that you are doing all these things for yourself – for someone who is worth the trouble, someone who is of value, the journey will become easier.

Good luck on your journey to restoring your spirit and reclaiming meaning, purpose, and joy in life!